RIDGWAY OF
MONTANA

STORY OF TO-DAY, IN WHICH
THE HERO IS ALSO THE VILLAIN

WILLIAM MACLEOD RAINE

1st WORLD
LIBRARY
Literary Society

Ridgway of Montana

William MacLeod Raine

© 1st World Library, 2008
PO Box 2211
Fairfield, IA 52556
www.1stworldlibrary.com
First Edition

LCCN: 2007908466

Softcover ISBN: 978-1-4218-9375-4
Hardcover ISBN: 978-1-4218-9475-1
eBook ISBN: 978-1-4218-9275-7

Purchase *"Ridgway of Montana"*
as a traditional bound book at:
www.1stWorldLibrary.com/purchase.asp?ISBN=978-1-4218-9375-4

1st World Library Literary Society

Giving Back to the World

"If you want to work on the core problem, it's early school literacy."

- James Barksdale, former CEO of Netscape

"No skill is more crucial to the future of a child, or to a democratic and prosperous society, than literacy."

- Los Angeles Times

"Literacy... means far more than learning how to read and write... The aim is to transmit... knowledge and promote social participation."

- UNESCO

"Literacy is not a luxury, it is a right and a responsibility. If our world is to meet the challenges of the twenty-first century we must harness the energy and creativity of all our citizens."

- President Bill Clinton

"Parents should be encouraged to read to their children, and teachers should be equipped with all available techniques for teaching literacy, so the varying needs and capacities of individual kids can be taken into account."

- Hugh Mackay

To JEAN

AND THAT KINGDOM

"Where you and I through this world's weather Work, and
give praise and thanks together."

WILLIAM MACLEOD RAINE

CONTENTS

CHAPTER 1

TWO MEN AND A WOMAN

"Mr. Ridgway, ma'am."

The young woman who was giving the last touches to the very effective picture framed in her long looking-glass nodded almost imperceptibly.

She had come to the parting of the ways, and she knew it, with a shrewd suspicion as to which she would choose. She had asked for a week to decide, and her heart-searching had told her nothing new. It was characteristic of Virginia Balfour that she did not attempt to deceive herself. If she married Waring Ridgway it would be for what she considered good and sufficient reasons, but love would not be one of them. He was going to be a great man, for one thing, and probably a very rich one, which counted, though it would not be a determining factor. This she could find only in the man himself, in the masterful force that made him what he was. The sandstings of life did not disturb his confidence in his victorious star, nor did he let fine-spun moral obligations hamper his predatory career. He had a genius for success in whatever he undertook, pushing his way to his end with a shrewd, direct energy that never faltered. She sometimes wondered whether she, too, like the men he used as tools, was merely a pawn in his game, and her consent an empty formality conceded to convention. Perhaps he would marry her even if she did not want to, she told herself, with the sudden illuminating smile that was one of her chief charms.

But Ridgway's wary eyes, appraising her mood as she came forward to meet him, read none of this doubt in her frank greeting. Anything more sure and exquisite than the cultivation Virginia Balfour breathed he would have been hard put to it to conceive. That her gown and its accessories seemed to him merely the extension of a dainty personality was the highest compliment he could pay her charm, and an entirely unconscious one.

"Have I kept you waiting?" she smiled, giving him her hand.

His answering smile, quite cool and unperturbed, gave the lie to his words. "For a year, though the almanac called it a week."

"You must have suffered," she told him ironically, with a glance at the clear color in his good-looking face.

"Repressed emotion," he explained. "May I hope that my suffering has reached a period?"

They had been sauntering toward a little conservatory at the end of the large room, but she deflected and brought up at a table on which lay some books. One of these she picked up and looked at incuriously for a moment before sweeping them aside. She rested her hands on the table behind her and leaned back against it, her eyes meeting his fairly.

"You're still of the same mind, are you?" she demanded.

"Oh! very much."

She lifted herself to the table, crossing her feet and dangling them irresponsibly. "We might as well be comfy while we talk;" and she indicated, by a nod, a chair.

"Thanks. If you don't mind, I think I'll take it standing."

She did not seem in any hurry to begin, and Ridgway gave evidence of no desire to hasten her. But presently he said, with a little laugh that seemed to offer her inclusion in the joke:

"I'm on the anxious seat, you know—waiting to find out whether I'm to be the happiest man alive."

"You know as much about it as I do." She echoed his laugh ruefully. "I'm still as much at sea as I was last week. I couldn't tell then, and I can't now."

"No news is good news, they say."

"I don't want to marry you a bit, but you're a great catch, as you are very well aware."

"I suppose I am rather a catch," he agreed, the shadow of a smile at the corners of his mouth.

"It isn't only your money; though, of course, that's a temptation," she admitted audaciously.

"I'm glad it's not only my money." He could laugh with her about it because he was shrewd enough to understand that it was not at all his wealth. Her cool frankness might have frightened away another man. It merely served to interest Ridgway. For, with all his strength, he was a vain man, always ready to talk of himself. He spent a good deal of his spare time interpreting himself to attractive and attracted young women.

Her gaze fastened on the tip of her suede toe, apparently studying it attentively. "It would be a gratification to my vanity to parade you as the captive of my bow and spear. You're such a magnificent specimen, such a berserk in broadcloth. Still. I shan't marry you if I can help it—but, then, I'm not sure that I can help it. Of course, I disapprove of you entirely, but you're rather fascinating, you know." Her eye traveled slowly up to his, appraising the masterful lines of his square figure, the dominant strength of his close-shut mouth and resolute eyes. "Perhaps 'fascinating' isn't just the word, but I can't help being interested in you, whether I like you or not. I suppose you always get what you want very badly?" she flung out by way of question.

"That's what I'm trying to discover"—he smiled.

"There are things to be considered both ways," she said, taking him into her confidence. "You trample on others. How do I know you wouldn't tread on me?"

"That would be one of the risks you would take," he agreed impersonally.

"I shouldn't like that at all. If I married you it would be because as your wife I should have so many opportunities. I should expect to do exactly as I please. I shouldn't want you to interfere with me, though I should want to be able to influence you."

"Nothing could be fairer than that," was his amiably ironical comment.

"You see, I don't know you—not really—and they say all sorts of things about you."

"They don't say I am a quitter, do they?"

She leaned forward, chin in hand and elbow on knee. It was a part of the accent of her distinction that as a rebel she was both demure and daring. "I wonder if I might ask you some questions—the intimate kind that people think but don't say—at least, they don't say them to you."

"It would be a pleasure to me to be put on the witness-stand. I should probably pick up some interesting side-lights about myself."

"Very well." Her eyes danced with excitement. "You're what they call a buccaneer of business, aren't you?"

Here were certainly diverting pastimes. "I believe I have been called that; but, then, I've had the hardest names in the dictionary thrown at me so often that I can't be sure."

"I suppose you are perfectly unscrupulous in a business way- stop at nothing to gain your point?"

He took her impudence smilingly.

"'Unscrupulous' isn't the word I use when I explain myself to myself, but as an unflattered description, such as one my enemies might use to describe me, I dare say it is fairly accurate."

"I wonder why. Do you dispense with a conscience entirely?"

"Well, you see, Miss Balfour, if I nursed a New England

conscience I could stand up to the attacks of the Consolidated about as long as a dove to a hawk. I meet fire with fire to avoid being wiped off the map of the mining world. I play the game. I can't afford to keep a button on my foil when my opponent doesn't."

She nodded an admission of his point. "And yet there are rules of the game to be observed, aren't there? The Consolidated people claim you steal their ore, I believe." Her slanted eyes studied the effect of her daring.

He laughed grimly. "Do they? I claim they steal mine. It's rather difficult to have an exact regard for mine and thine before the courts decide which is which."

"And meanwhile, in order to forestall an adverse decision, you are working extra shifts to get all the ore out of the disputed veins."

"Precisely, just as they are," he admitted dryly. "Then the side that loses will not be so disappointed, since the value of the veins will be less. Besides, stealing ore openly doesn't count. It is really a moral obligation in a fight like this," he explained.

"A moral obligation?"

"Exactly. You can't hit a trust over the head with the decalogue. Modern business is war. Somebody is bound to get hurt. If I win out it will be because I put up a better fight than the Consolidated, and cripple it enough to make it let me alone. I'm looking out for myself, and I don't pretend to be any better than my neighbors. When you get down to bed-rock honesty, I've never seen it in business. We're all of us as honest as we think we can afford to be. I haven't noticed that there is any premium on it in Mesa. Might makes right. I'll win if I'm strong enough; I'll fail if I'm not. That's the law of life. I didn't make this strenuous little world, and I'm not responsible for it. If I play I have to take the rules the way they are, not the way I should like them to be. I'm not squeamish, and I'm not a hypocrite. Simon Harley isn't squeamish, either, but he happens to be a hypocrite. So there you have the difference between us."

The president of the Mesa Ore-producing Company set forth his creed jauntily, without the least consciousness of need for apology for the fact that it happened to be divorced from morality. Its frank disregard of ethical considerations startled Miss Balfour without shocking her. She liked his candor, even though it condemned him. It was really very nice of him to take her impudence so well. He certainly wasn't a prig, anyway.

"And morality," she suggested tentatively.

"—hasn't a thing to do with success, the parsons to the contrary notwithstanding. The battle is to the strong."

"Then the Consolidated will beat you finally."

He smiled. "They would if I'd let them; but brains and resource and finesse all count for power. Granted that they have a hundred dollars to my one. Still, I have elements of strength they can't even estimate. David beat Goliath, you know, even though he didn't do it with a big stick."

"So you think morality is for old women?"

"And young women," he amended, smiling.

"And every man is to be a law unto himself?"

"Not quite. Some men aren't big enough to be. Let them stick to the conventional code. For me, if I make my own laws I don't break them."

"And you're sure that you're on the road to true success?" she asked lightly.

"Now, you have heaven in the back of your mind."

"Not exactly," she laughed. "But I didn't expect you to understand."

"Then I won't disappoint you," he said cheerfully.

She came back to the concrete.

"I should like to know whether it is true that you own the courts of Yuba County and have the decisions of the judges written at your lawyer's offices in cases between you and the Consolidated."

"If I do," he answered easily, "I am doing just what the Consolidated would do in case they had been so fortunate as to have won the last election and seated their judicial candidates. One expects a friendly leaning from the men one put in office."

"Isn't the judiciary supposed to be the final, incorruptible bulwark of the nation?" she pretended to want to know.

"I believe it is supposed to be."

"Isn't it rather—loading the dice, to interfere with the courts?"

"I find the dice already loaded. I merely substitute others of my own."

"You don't seem a bit ashamed of yourself."

"I'm ashamed of the Consolidated"—he smiled.

"That's a comfortable position to be able to take." She fixed him for a moment with her charming frown of interrogation. "You won't mind my asking these questions? I'm trying to decide whether you are too much of a pirate for me. Perhaps when I've made up my mind you won't want me," she added.

"Oh, I'll want you!" Then coolly: "Shall we wait till you make up your mind before announcing the engagement?"

"Don't be too sure," she flashed at him.

"I'm horribly unsure."

"Of course, you're laughing at me, just as you would"—she tilted a sudden sideways glance at him—"if I asked you WHY you wanted to marry me."

"Oh, if you take me that way—"

She interrupted airily. "I'm trying to make up my mind whether to take you at all."

"You certainly have a direct way of getting at things."

He studied appreciatively her piquant, tilted face; the long, graceful lines of her slender, perfect figure. "I take it you don't want the sentimental reason for my wishing to marry you, though I find that amply justified. But if you want another, you must still look to yourself for it. My business leads me to appreciate values correctly. When I desire you to sit at the head of my table, to order my house, my judgment justifies itself. I have a fancy always for the best. When I can't gratify it I do without."

"Thank you." She made him a gay little mock curtsy "I had heard you were no carpet-knight, Mr. Ridgway. But rumor is a lying jade, for I am being told—am I not?—that in case I don't take pity on you, the lone future of a celibate stretches drear before you."

"Oh, certainly."

Having come to the end of that passage, she tried another. "A young man told me yesterday you were a fighter. He said he guessed you would stand the acid. What did he mean?"

Ridgway was an egoist from head to heel. He could voice his own praises by the hour when necessary, but now he sidestepped her little trap to make him praise himself at secondhand.

"Better ask him."

"ARE you a fighter, then?"

Had he known her and her whimsies less well, he might have taken her audacity for innocence.

"One couldn't lie down, you know."

"Of course, you always fight fair," she mocked.

"When a fellow's attacked by a gang of thugs he doesn't pray for boxing-gloves. He lets fly with a coupling-pin if that's what comes handy."

Her eyes, glinting sparks of mischief, marveled at him with mock reverence, but she knew in her heart that her mockery was a fraud. She did admire him; admired him even while she disapproved the magnificent lawlessness of him.

For Waring Ridgway looked every inch the indomitable fighter he was. He stood six feet to the line, straight and strong, carrying just sufficient bulk to temper his restless energy without impairing its power. Nor did the face offer any shock of disappointment to the promise given by the splendid figure. Salient-jawed and forceful, set with cool, flinty, blue-gray eyes, no place for weakness could be found there. One might have read a moral callousness, a colorblindness in points of rectitude, but when the last word had been said, its masterful capability, remained the outstanding impression.

"Am I out of the witness-box?" he presently asked, still leaning against the mantel from which he had been watching her impersonally as an intellectual entertainment.

"I think so."

"And the verdict?"

"You know what it ought to be," she accused.

"Fortunately, kisses go by favor, not by, merit."

"You don't even make a pretense of deserving."

"Give me credit for being an honest rogue, at least."

"But a rogue?" she insisted lightly.

"Oh, a question of definitions. I could make a very good case for myself as an honest man."

"If you thought it worth while?"

"If I didn't happen to want to be square with you"—he smiled.

"You're so fond of me, I suppose, that you couldn't bear to have me think too well of you."

"You know how fond of you I am."

"Yes, it is a pity about you," she scoffed.

"Believe me, yes," he replied cheerfully.

She drummed with her pink finger-tips on her chin, studying him meditatively. To do him justice, she had to admit that he did not even pretend much. He wanted her because she was a step up in the social ladder, and, in his opinion, the most attractive girl he knew. That he was not in love with her relieved the situation, as Miss Balfour admitted to herself in impersonal moods. But there were times when she could have wished he were. She felt it to be really due her attractions that his pulses should quicken for her, and in the interests of experience she would have liked to see how he would make love if he really meant it from the heart and not the will.

"It's really an awful bother," she sighed.

"Referring to the little problem of your future?"

"Yes."

"Can't make up your mind whether I come in?"

"No." She looked up brightly, with an effect of impulsiveness. "I don't suppose you want to give me another week?"

"A reprieve! But why? You're going to marry me."

"I suppose so." She laughed. "I wish I could have my cake, and eat it, too."

"It would be a moral iniquity to encourage such a system of ethics."

"So you won't give me a week?" she sighed. "All sorts of things might have happened in that week. I shall always believe that the fairy prince would have come for me."

"Believe that he HAS come," he claimed.

"Oh, I didn't mean a prince of pirates, though there is a triumph in having tamed a pirate chief to prosaic matrimony. In one way it will be a pity, too. You won't be half so picturesque. You remember how Stevenson puts it: 'that marriage takes from a man the capacity for great things, whether good or bad.'"

"I can stand a good deal of taming."

"Domesticating a pirate ought to be an interesting process," she conceded, her rare smile flashing. "It should prove a cure for ENNUI, but then I'm never a victim of that malady."

"Am I being told that I am to be the happiest pirate alive?"

"I expect you are."

His big hand gripped hers till it tingled. She caught his eye on a roving quest to the door.

"We don't have to do that," she announced hurriedly, with an embarrassed flush.

"I don't do it because I have to," he retorted, kissing her on the lips.

She fell back, protesting. "Under the circumstances—"

The butler, with a card on a tray, interrupted silently. She glanced at the card, devoutly grateful his impassive majesty's entrance had not been a moment earlier.

"Show him in here."

"The fairy prince, five minutes too late?" asked Ridgway, when the man had gone.

For answer she handed him the card, yet he thought the pink that flushed her cheek was something more pronounced than usual. But he was willing to admit there might be a choice of reasons for that.

"Lyndon Hobart" was the name he read.

"I think the Consolidated is going to have its innings. I should like to stay, of course, but I fear I must plead a subsequent engagement and leave the field to the enemy."

Pronouncing "Mr. Hobart" without emphasis, the butler vanished. The newcomer came forward with the quiet assurance of the born aristocrat. He was a slender, well-knit man, dressed fastidiously, with clear-cut, classical features; cool, keen eyes, and a gentle, you-be-damned manner to his inferiors. Beside him Ridgway bulked too large, too florid. His ease seemed a little obvious, his prosperity overemphasized. Even his voice, strong and reliant, lacked the tone of gentle blood that Hobart had inherited with his nice taste.

When Miss Balfour said: "I think you know each other," the manager of the Consolidated bowed with stiff formality, but his rival laughed genially and said: "Oh, yes, I know Mr. Hobart." The geniality was genuine enough, but through it ran a note of contempt. Hobart read in it a veiled taunt. To him it seemed to say

"Yes, I have met him, and beaten him at every turn of the road, though he has been backed by a power with resources a hundred times as great as mine."

In his parting excuses to Miss Balfour, Ridgway's audacity crystallized in words that Hobart could only regard as a shameless challenge. "I regret that an appointment with Judge Purcell necessitates my leaving such good company," he said urbanely.

Purcell was the judge before whom was pending a suit between the Consolidated and the Mesa Ore-producing Company, to determine the ownership of the Never Say Die Mine; and it was current report that Ridgway owned him as absolutely as he did the automobile waiting for him now at the door.

If Ridgway expected his opponent to pay his flippant gibe the honor of repartee, he was disappointed. To be sure, Hobart, admirably erect in his slender grace, was moved to a slight, disdainful smile, but it evidenced scarcely the appreciation that anybody less impervious to criticism than Ridgway would have cared to see.

CHAPTER 2

THE FREEBOOTER

When next Virginia Balfour saw Waring Ridgway she was driving her trap down one of the hit-or-miss streets of Mesa, where derricks, shaft-houses, and gray slag-dumps shoulder ornate mansions conglomerate of many unharmonious details of architecture. To Miss Balfour these composites and their owners would have been joys unalloyed except for the microbe of society ambition that was infecting the latter, and transforming them from simple, robust, self-reliant Westerners into a class of servile, nondescript newly rich, that resembled their unfettered selves as much as tame bears do the grizzlies of their own Rockies. As she had once complained smilingly to Hobart, she had not come to the West to study ragged edges of the social fringe. She might have done that in New York.

Virginia was still a block or two from the court-house on the hill, when it emptied into the street a concourse of excited men. That this was an occasion of some sort it was easy to guess, and of what sort she began to have an inkling, when Ridgway came out, the center of a circle of congratulating admirers. She was obliged to admit that he accepted their applause without in the least losing his head. Indeed, he took it as imperturbably as did Hobart, against whom a wave of

William MacLeod Raine

the enthusiasm seemed to be directed in the form of a jeer, when he passed down the steps with Mott, one of the Consolidated lawyers. Miss Balfour timed her approach to meet Hobart at a right angle.

"What is it all about?" she asked, after he had reached her side.

"Judge Purcell has just decided the Never Say Die case in favor of Mr. Ridgway and against the Consolidated."

"Is that a great victory for him?"

"Yes, it's a victory, though, of course, we appeal," admitted Hobart. "But we can't say we didn't expect it," he added cheerfully.

"Mayn't I give you a lift if you are going down-town?" she said quickly, for Ridgway, having detached himself from the group, was working toward her, and she felt an instinctive sympathy for the man who had lost. Furthermore, she had something she wanted to tell him before he heard it on the tongue of rumor.

"Since you are so kind;" and he climbed to the place beside her.

"Congratulate me, Miss Balfour," demanded Ridgway, as he shook hands with her, nodding coolly at her companion. "I'm a million dollars richer than I was an hour ago. I have met the enemy and he is mine."

Virginia, resenting the bad taste of his jeer at the man who sat beside her, misunderstood him promptly. "Did you say you had met the enemy and won his mine?"

He laughed. "You're a good one!"

"Thank you very much for this unsolicited testimonial," she said gravely. "In the meantime, to avoid a congestion of traffic, we'll be moving, if you will kindly give me back my front left wheel."

He did not lift his foot from the spoke on which it rested. "My congratulations," he reminded her.

"I wish you all the joy in your victory that you deserve, and I hope the supreme court will reaffirm the decision of Judge Purcell, if it is a just one," was the form in which she acceded to his demand.

She flicked her whip, and Ridgway fell back, laughing. "You've been subsidized by the Consolidated," he shouted after her.

Hobart watched silently the businesslike directness with which the girl handled the ribbons. She looked every inch the thoroughbred in her well-made covert coat and dainty driving gauntlets. The grace of the alert, slender figure, the perfect poise of the beautiful little tawny head, proclaimed her distinction no less certainly than the fine modeling of the mobile face. It was a distinction that stirred the pulse of his emotion and disarmed his keen, critical sense. Ridgway could study her with an amused, detached interest, but Hobart's admiration had traveled past that point. He found it as impossible to define her charm as to evade it. Her inheritance of blood and her environment should have made her a finished product of civilization, but her salty breeziness, her nerve, vivid as a flame at times, disturbed delightfully the poise that held her when in repose.

When Virginia spoke, it was to ask abruptly: "Is it really

his mine?"

"Judge Purcell says so."

"But do YOU think so—down in the bottom of your heart?"

"Wouldn't I naturally be prejudiced?"

"I suppose you would. Everybody in Mesa seems to have taken sides either with Mr. Ridgway or the Consolidated. Still, you have an option. Is he what his friends proclaim him—the generous-hearted independent fighting against trust domination? Or is he merely an audacious ore-thief, as his enemies say? The truth must be somewhere."

"It seems to lie mostly in point of view here the angle of observation being determined by interest," he answered.

"And from your angle of observation?"

"He is the most unusual man I ever saw, the most resourceful and the most competent. He never knows when he is beaten. I suppose that's the reason he never is beaten finally. We have driven him to the wall a score of times. My experience with him is that he's most dangerous when one thinks he must be about hammered out. He always hits back then in the most daring and unexpected way."

"With a coupling-pin," she suggested with a little reminiscent laugh.

"Metaphorically speaking. He reaches for the first effective weapon to his hand."

"You haven't quite answered my question yet," she reminded him. "Is he what his friends or what his enemies think him?"

"If you ask me I can only say that I'm one of his enemies."

"But a fair-minded man," she replied quickly.

"Thank you. Then I'll say that perhaps he is neither just what his friends or his foes think him. One must make allowances for his training and temperament, and for that quality of bigness in him. 'Mediocre men go soberly on the highroads, but saints and scoundrels meet in the jails,'" he smilingly quoted.

"He would make a queer sort of saint," she laughed.

"A typical twentieth century one of a money-mad age."

She liked it in him that he would not use the opportunity she had made to sneer at his adversary, none the less because she knew that Ridgway might not have been so scrupulous in his place. That Lyndon Hobart's fastidious instincts for fair play had stood in the way of his success in the fight to down Ridgway she had repeatedly heard. Of late, rumors had persisted in reporting dissatisfaction with his management of the Consolidated at the great financial center on Broadway which controlled the big copper company. Simon Harley, the dominating factor in the octopus whose tentacles reached out in every direction to monopolize the avenues of wealth, demanded of his subordinates results. Methods were no concern of his, and failure could not be explained to him. He wanted Ridgway crushed, and the pulse of the copper production regulated lay the Consolidated. Instead, he had seen Ridgway rise steadily to power and wealth despite his efforts to wipe him off the slate. Hobart was perfectly aware that his head was likely to fall when Harley heard of Purcell's decision in regard to the Never Say Die.

"He certainly is an amazing man," Virginia mused, her

fiancee in mind. "It would be interesting to discover what he can't do—along utilitarian lines, I mean. Is he as good a miner underground as he is in the courts?" she flung out.

"He is the shrewdest investor I know. Time and again he has leased or bought apparently worthless claims, and made them pay inside of a few weeks. Take the Taurus as a case in point. He struck rich ore in a fortnight. Other men had done development work for years and found nothing."

"I'm naturally interested in knowing all about him, because I have just become engaged to him," explained Miss Virginia, as calmly as if her pulse were not fluttering a hundred to the minute

Virginia was essentially a sportsman. She did not flinch from the guns when the firing was heavy. It had been remarked of her even as a child that she liked to get unpleasant things over with as soon as possible, rather than postpone them. Once, *aetat* eight, she had marched in to her mother like a stoic and announced: "I've come to be whipped, momsie, 'cause I broke that horrid little Nellie Vaile's doll. I did it on purpose, 'cause I was mad at her. I'm glad I broke it, so there!"

Hobart paled slightly beneath his outdoors Western tan, but his eyes met hers very steadily and fairly. "I wish you happiness, Miss Balfour, from the bottom of my heart."

She nodded a brisk "Thank you," and directed her attention again to the horses.

"Take him by and large, Mr. Ridgway is the most capable, energetic, and far-sighted business man I have ever known. He has a bigger grasp of things than almost any financier in the country. I think you'll find he will go far," he said, choosing his words with care to say as much for Waring Ridgway as he honestly could.

"I have always thought so," agreed Virginia.

She had reason for thinking so in that young man's remarkable career. When Waring Ridgway had first come to Mesa he had been a draftsman for the Consolidated at five dollars a day. He was just out of Cornell, and his assets consisted mainly of a supreme confidence in himself and an imposing presence. He was a born leader, and he flung himself into the raw, turbid life of the mining town with a readiness that had not a little to do with his subsequent success.

That success began to take tangible form almost from the first. A small, independent smelter that had for long been working at a loss was about to fall into the hands of the Consolidated when Ridgway bought it on promises to pay, made good by raising money on a flying trip he took to the East. His father died about this time and left him fifty thousand dollars, with which he bought the Taurus, a mine in which several adventurous spirits had dropped small fortunes. He acquired other properties; a lease here, an interest there. It began to be observed that he bought always with judgment. He seemed to have the touch of Midas. Where other men had lost money he made it.

When the officers of the Consolidated woke up to the menace of his presence, one of their lawyers called on him. The agent of the Consolidated smiled at his luxurious offices, which looked more like a woman's boudoir than the business place of a Western miner. But that was merely part of Ridgway's vanity, and did not in the least interfere with his predatory instincts. Many people who walked into that parlor to do business played fly to his spider.

The lawyer had been ready to patronize the upstart who had ventured so boldly into the territory of the great trust, but one glance at the clear-cut resolute face of the young man changed his mind.

"I've come to make you an offer for your smelter, Mr. Ridgway," he began. "We'll take it off your hands at the price it cost you."

"Not for sale, Mr. Bartel."

"Very well. We'll give you ten thousand more than you paid for it."

"You misunderstand me. It is not for sale."

"Oh, come! You bought it to sell to us. What can you do with it?"

"Run it," suggested Ridgway.

"Without ore?"

"You forget that I own a few properties, and have leases on others. When the Taurus begins producing, I'll have enough to keep the smelter going."

"When the Taurus begins producing?"—Bartel smiled skeptically. "Didn't Johnson and Leroy drop fortunes on that expectation?"

"I'll bet five thousand dollars we make a strike within two weeks."

"Chimerical!" pronounced the graybeard as he rose to go, with an air of finality. "Better sell the smelter while you have the chance."

"Think not," disagreed Ridgway.

At the door the lawyer turned. "Oh, there's another matter! It had slipped my mind." He spoke with rather elaborate carelessness. "It seems that there is a little triangle—about ten and four feet across—wedged in between the Mary K, the Diamond King, and the Marcus Daly. For some reason we accidentally omitted to file on it. Our chief engineer finds that you have taken it up, Mr. Ridgway. It is really of no value, but it is in the heart of our properties, and so it ought to belong to us. Of course, it is of no use to you. There isn't any possible room to sink a shaft. We'll take it from you if you like, and even pay you a nominal price. For what will you sell?"

Ridgway lit a cigar before he answered: "One million dollars."

"What?" screamed Bartel.

"Not a cent less. I call it the Trust Buster. Before I'm through, you'll find it is worth that to me."

The lawyer reported him demented to the Consolidated officials, who declared war on him from that day.

They found the young adventurer more than prepared for them. If he had a Napoleonic sense of big vital factors, he had no less a genius for detail. He had already picked up an intimate knowledge of the hundreds of veins and crossveins that traverse the Mesa copper-fields, and he had delved patiently into the tangled history of the litigation that the defective mining laws in pioneer days had made possible. When the Consolidated attempted to harass him by legal process, he countered by instituting a score of suits against the company within the week. These had to do with wills, insanity cases, extra lateral rights, mine titles, and land and water rights. Wherever Ridgway saw room for an entering wedge to dispute the title of the Consolidated, he drove a new suit home. To say the least, the trust found it annoying to be enjoined from working its mines, to be cited for contempt before judges employed in the interests of its opponent, to be served with restraining orders when clearly within its rights. But when these adverse legal decisions began to affect vital issues, the Consolidated looked for reasons why Ridgway should control the courts. It found them in politics.

For Ridgway was already dominating the politics of Yuba County, displaying an amazing acumen and a surprising ability as a stumpspeaker. He posed as a friend of the people, an enemy of the trust. He declared an eight-hour day for his own miners, and called upon the Consolidated to do the same. Hobart refused, acting on orders from Broadway, and fifteen thousand Consolidated miners went to the polls and reelected Ridgway's corrupt judges, in spite of the fight the Consolidated was making against them.

Meanwhile, Ridgway's colossal audacity made the Consolidated's copper pay for the litigation with which he was harassing it. In following his ore-veins, or what he claimed to be his veins, he crossed boldly into the territory of the enemy. By the law of extra lateral rights, a man is entitled to mine within the lines of other property than his own, provided he is following the dip of a vein which has its apex in his claim. Ridgway's experts were prepared to swear that all the best veins in the field apexed in his property. Pending decisions of the courts, they assumed it, tunneling through granite till they tapped the veins of the Consolidated mines, meanwhile enjoining that company from working the very ore of which Ridgway was robbing it.

Many times the great trust back of the Consolidated had him close to ruin, but Ridgway's alert brain and supreme audacity carried him through. From their mines or from his own he always succeeded in extracting enough ore to meet his obligations when they fell due. His powerful enemy, as Hobart had told Miss Balfour, found him most dangerous when it seemed to have him with his back to the wall. Then unexpectedly would fall some crushing blow that put the financial kings of Broadway on the defensive long enough for him to slip out of the corner into which they had driven him. Greatly daring, he had the successful cavalryman's instinct of risking much to gain much. A gambler, his enemies characterized him fitly enough. But it was also true, as Mesa phrased it, that he gambled "with the lid off," playing for large stakes, neither asking nor giving quarter.

At the end of five years of desperate fighting, the freebooter was more strongly entrenched than he had been at any previous time. The railroads, pledged to give rebates to the Consolidated, had been forced by Ridgway, under menace of adverse legislation from the men he controlled at the State-house, to give him secretly a still better rate than the trust. He owned the county courts, he was supported by the people, and had become a political dictator, and the financial outlook for him grew brighter every day.

Such were the conditions when Judge Purcell handed down his Never Say Die decision. Within an hour Hobart was reading a telegram in cipher from the Broadway head-quarters. It announced the immediate departure for Mesa of the great leader of the octopus. Simon Harley, the Napoleon of finance, was coming out to attend personally to the destruction of the buccaneer who had dared to fire on the trust flag.

Before night some one of his corps of spies in the employ of the enemy carried the news to Waring Ridgway. He smiled grimly, his bluegray eyes hardening to the temper of steel. Here at last was a foeman worthy of his metal; one as lawless, unscrupulous, daring, and far-seeing as himself, with a hundred times his resources.

CHAPTER 3

ONE TO ONE

The solitary rider stood for a moment in silhouette against the somber sky-line, his keen eyes searching the lowering clouds.

"Getting its back up for a blizzard," he muttered to himself, as he touched his pony with the spur.

Dark, heavy billows banked in the west, piling over each other as they drove forward. Already the advance-guard had swept the sunlight from the earth, except for a flutter of it that still protested near the horizon. Scattering snowflakes were flying, and even in a few minutes the temperature had fallen many degrees.

The rider knew the signs of old. He recognized the sudden stealthy approach that transformed a sun-drenched, friendly plain into an unknown arctic waste. Not for nothing had he been last year one of a search-party to find the bodies of three miners frozen to death not fifty yards from their own cabin. He understood perfectly what it meant to be caught away from shelter when the driven white pall wiped out distance and direction; made long familiar landmarks strange, and numbed the will to a helpless surrender. The knowledge of it was spur enough to make him ride fast while he still retained the sense of direction.

But silently, steadily, the storm increased, and he was forced to slacken his pace. As the blinding snow grew thick, the sound of the wind deadened, unable to penetrate the dense white wall through which he forced his way. The world narrowed to a space whose boundaries he could touch with his extended hands. In this white mystery that wrapped him, nothing was left but stinging snow, bitter cold, and the silence of the dead.

So he thought one moment, and the next was almost flung by his swerving horse into a vehicle that blocked the road. Its blurred outlines presently resolved themselves into an automobile, crouched in the bottom of which was an inert huddle of humanity.

He shouted, forgetting that no voice could carry through the muffled scream of the storm. When he got no answer, he guided his horse close to the machine and reached down to snatch away the rug already heavy with snow. To his surprise, it was a girl's despairing face that looked up at him. She tried to rise, but fell back, her muscles too numb to serve.

"Don't leave me," she implored, stretching her, arms toward him.

He reached out and lifted her to his horse. "Are you alone?"

"Yes. He went for help when the machine broke down— before the storm," she sobbed. He had to put his ear to her mouth to catch the words.

"Come, keep up your heart." There was that in his voice

pealed like a trumpet-call to her courage.

"I'm freezing to death," she moaned.

She was exhausted and benumbed, her lips blue, her flesh gray. It was plain to him that she had reached the limit of endurance, that she was ready to sink into the last torpor. He ripped open his overcoat and shook the snow from it, then gathered her close so that she might get the warmth of his body. The rugs from the automobile he wrapped round them both.

"Courage!" he cried. "There's a miner's cabin near. Don't give up, child."

But his own courage was of the heart and will, not of the head. He had small hope of reaching the hut at the entrance of Dead Man's Gulch or, if he could struggle so far, of finding it in the white swirl that clutched at them. Near and far are words not coined for a blizzard. He might stagger past with safety only a dozen feet from him. He might lie down and die at the very threshold of the door. Or he might wander in an opposite direction and miss the cabin by a mile.

Yet it was not in the man to give up. He must stagger on till he could no longer stand. He must fight so long as life was in him. He must crawl forward, though his forlorn hope had vanished. And he did. When the worn-out horse slipped down and could not be coaxed to its feet again, he picked up the bundle of rugs and plowed forward blindly, soul and body racked, but teeth still set fast with the primal instinct never to give up. The intense cold of the air, thick with gray sifted ice, searched the warmth from his body and sapped his vitality. His numbed legs doubled under him like springs. He was down and up again a dozen times, but always the call of life drove him on, dragging his helpless burden with him.

That he did find the safety of the cabin in the end was due to no wisdom on his part. He had followed unconsciously the dip of the ground that led him into the little draw where it had been built, and by sheer luck stumbled against it. His strength was gone, but the door gave to his weight, and he buckled across the threshold like a man helpless with drink. He dropped to the floor, ready to sink into a stupor, but he shook sleep from him and dragged himself to his feet. Presently his numb fingers found a match, a newspaper, and some wood. As soon as he had control over his hands, he fell to chafing hers. He slipped off her dainty shoes, pathetically inadequate for such an experience, and rubbed her feet back to feeling. She had been torpid, but when the blood began to circulate, she cried out in agony at the pain.

Every inch of her bore the hall-mark of wealth. The ermine-lined motoring-cloak, the broadcloth cut on simple lines of elegance, the quality of her lingerie and of the hosiery which incased the wonderfully small feet, all told of a padded existence from which the cares of life had been excluded. The satin flesh he massaged, to renew the flow of the dammed blood, was soft and tender like a babe's. Quite surely she was an exotic, the last woman in the world fitted for the hardships of this frontier country. She had none of the deep-breasted vitality of those of her sex who have fought with grim nature and won. His experience told him that a very little longer in the storm would have snuffed out the wick of her life.

But he knew, too, that the danger was past. Faint tints of pink were beginning to warm the cheeks that had been so deathly pallid. Already crimson lips were offering a vivid contrast to the still, almost colorless face.

For she was biting the little lips to try and keep back the cries of pain that returning life wrung from her. Big tears coursed down her cheeks, and broken sobs caught her breath. She was helpless as an infant before the searching pain that wracked her

"I can't stand it—I can't stand it," she moaned, and in her distress stretched out her little hand for relief as a baby might to its mother.

The childlike appeal of the flinching violet eyes in the tortured face moved him strangely. He was accounted a hard man, not without reason. His eyes were those of a gambler, cold and vigilant. It was said that he could follow an undeviating course without relenting at the ruin and misery wrought upon others by his operations. But the helpless loveliness of this exquisitely dainty child-woman, the sense of intimacy bred of a common peril endured, of the strangeness of their environment and of her utter dependence upon him, carried the man out of himself and away from conventions.

He stooped and gathered her into his arms, walking the floor with her and cheering her as if she had indeed been the child they both for the moment conceived her.

"You don't know how it hurts," she pleaded between sobs, looking up into the strong face so close to hers.

"I know it must, dear. But soon it will be better. Every twinge is one less, and shows that you are getting well. Be brave for just a few minutes more now."

She smiled wanly through her tears. "But I'm not brave. I'm a little coward—and it does pain so."

"I know—I know. It is dreadful. But just a few minutes now."

"You're good to me," she said presently, simply as a little girl might have said it.

To neither of them did it seem strange that she should be there in his arms, her fair head against his shoulder, nor that she should cling convulsively to him when the fierce pain tingled unbearably. She had reached out for the nearest help, and he gave of his strength and courage abundantly.

Presently the prickling of the flowing blood grew less sharp. She began to grow drowsy with warmth after the fatigue and pain. The big eyes shut, fluttered open, smiled at him, and again closed. She had fallen asleep from sheer exhaustion.

He looked down with an odd queer feeling at the small aristocratic face relaxed upon his ann. The long lashes had drooped to the cheeks and shuttered the eyes that had met his with such confident appeal, but they did not hide the dark rings underneath, born of the hardships she had endured. As he walked the floor with her, he lived once more the terrible struggle through which they had passed. He saw Death stretching out icy hands for her, and as his arms unconsciously tightened about the soft rounded body, his square jaw set and the fighting spark leaped to his eyes.

"No, by Heaven," he gave back aloud his defiance.

Troubled dreams pursued her in her sleep. She clung close to him, her arm creeping round his neck for safety. He was a man not given to fine scruples, but all the best in him responded to her unconscious trust.

It was so she found herself when she awakened, stiff from her cramped position. She slipped at once to the floor and sat there drying her lace skirts, the sweet piquancy of her childish face set out by the leaping fire-glow that lit and shadowed her delicate coloring. Outside in the gray darkness raged the death from which he had snatched her by a miracle. Beyond—a million miles away—the world whose claim had loosened on them was going through its routine of lies and love, of hypocrisies and heroisms. But here were just they two, flung back to the primordial type by the fierce battle for existence that had encompassed them—Adam and Eve in the garden, one to one, all else forgot, all other ties and obligations for the moment obliterated. Had they not struggled, heart beating against heart, with the breath of death icing them, and come out alive? Was their world not contracted to a space ten feet by twelve, shut in from every other planet by an illimitable stretch of storm?

"Where should I have been if you had not found me?" she murmured, her haunting eyes fixed on the flames.

"But I should have found you—no matter where you had been, I should have found you."

The words seemed to leap from him of themselves. He was sure he had not meant to speak them, to voice so soon the claim that seemed to him so natural and reasonable.

She considered his words and found delight in acquiescing at once. The unconscious demand for life, for love, of her starved soul had never been gratified. But he had come to her through that fearful valley of death, because he must, because it had always been meant he should.

Her lustrous eyes, big with faith, looked up and met his.

The far, wise voices of the world were storm-deadened. They cried no warning to these drifting hearts. How should they know in that moment when their souls reached toward each other that the wisdom of the ages had decreed their yearning futile?

CHAPTER 4

TORT SALVATION

She must have fallen asleep there, for when she opened her eyes it was day. Underneath her was a lot of bedding he had found in the cabin, and tucked about her were the automobile rugs. For a moment her brain, still sodden with sleep, struggled helplessly with her surroundings. She looked at the smoky rafters without understanding, and her eyes searched the cabin wonderingly for her maid. When she remembered, her first thought was to look for the man. That he had gone, she saw with instinctive terror.

But not without leaving a message. She found his penciled note, weighted for security by a dollar, at the edge of the hearth.

"Gone on a foraging expedition. Back in an hour, Little Partner," was all it said. The other man also had promised to be back in an hour, and he had not come, but the strong chirography of the note, recalling the resolute strength of this man's face, brought content to her eyes. He had said he would come back. She rested secure in that pledge.

She went to the window and looked out over the great white wastes that rose tier on tier to the dull sky-line. She shuddered at the arctic desolation of the vast snow-fields. The mountains were sheeted with silence and purity. It seemed to the untaught child-woman that she was face to face with the Almighty.

Once during the night she had partially awakened to hear the roaring wind as it buffeted snow-clouds across the range. It had come tearing along the divide with the black storm in its vanguard, and she had heard fearfully the shrieks and screams of the battle as it raged up and down the gulches and sifted into them the deep drifts.

Half-asleep as she was, she had been afraid and had cried out with terror at this strange wakening; and he had been beside her in an instant.

"It's all right, partner. There's nothing to be afraid of," he had said cheerfully, taking her little hand in his big warm one.

Her fears had slipped away at once. Nestling down into her rug, she had smiled sleepily at him and fallen asleep with her cheek on her hand, her other hand still in his.

While she had been asleep the snow-tides had filled the gulch, had risen level with the top of the lower pane of the window. Nothing broke the smoothness of its flow save the one track he had made in breaking a way out. That he should have tried to find his way through such an untracked desolation amazed her. He could never do it. No puny human atom could fight successfully against the barriers nature had dropped so sullenly to fence them. They were set off from the world by a quarantine of God. There was something awful to her in the knowledge. It emphasized their impotence. Yet, this man had set himself to fight the inevitable.

With a little shudder she turned from the window to the

cheerless room. The floor was dirty; unwashed dishes were piled upon the table. Here and there were scattered muddy boots and overalls, just as their owner, the prospector, had left them before he had gone to the nearest town to restock his exhausted supply of provisions. Disorder and dirt filled the rough cabin, or so it seemed to her fastidious eye.

The inspiration of the housewife seized her. She would surprise him on his return by opening the door to him upon a house swept and garnished. She would show him that she could be of some use even in such a primitive topsy-turvy world as this into which Fate had thrust her willy-nilly.

First, she carried red live coals on a shovel from the fireplace to the cook-stove, and piled kindling upon them till it lighted. It was a new experience to her. She knew nothing of housework; had never lit a fire in her life, except once when she had been one of a camping party. The smoke choked her before she had the lids back in their places, but despite her awkwardness, the girl went about her unaccustomed tasks with a light heart. It was for her new-found hero that she played at housekeeping. For his commendation she filled the tea-kettle, enveloped herself in a cloud of dust as she wielded the stub of a broom she discovered, and washed the greasy dishes after the water was hot. A childish pleasure suffused her. All her life her least whims had been ministered to; she was reveling in a first attempt at service. As she moved to and fro with an improvised dust-rag, sunshine filled her being. From her lips the joy notes fell in song, shaken from her throat for sheer happiness. This surely was life, that life from which she had so carefully been hedged all the years of her young existence.

As he came down the trail he had broken, with a pack on his back, the man heard her birdlike carol in the clear frosty air. He emptied his chest in a deep shout, and she was instantly at the window, waving him a welcome with her dust-rag.

"I thought you were never coming," she cried from the open door as he came up the path.

Her eyes were starry in their eagerness. Every sensitive feature was alert with interest, so that the man thought he had never seen so mobile and attractive a face.

"Did it seem long?" he asked.

"Oh, weeks and weeks! You must be frozen to an icicle. Come in and get warm."

"I'm as warm as toast," he assured her.

He was glowing with exercise and the sting of the cold, for he had tramped two miles through drifts from three to five feet deep, battling with them every step of the way, and carrying with him on the return trip a box of provisions.

"With all that snow on you and the pack on your back, it's like Santa Claus," she cried, clapping her hands.

"Before we're through with the adventure we may think that box a sure enough gift from Santa," he replied.

After he had put it down, he took off his overcoat on the threshold and shook the snow from it. Then, with much feet stamping and scattering of snow, he came in. She fluttered about him, dragging a chair up to the fire for him, and taking his hat and gloves. It amused and pleased him that she should be so solicitous, and he surrendered himself to her ministrations.

His quick eye noticed the swept floor and the evanishment of disorder. "Hello! What's this clean through a fall house-cleaning? I'm not the only member of the firm that has been working. Dishes washed, floor swept, bed made, kitchen fire lit. You've certainly been going some, unless the fairies helped you. Aren't you afraid of blistering these little hands?" he asked gaily, taking one of them in his and touching the soft palm gently with the tip of his finger.

"I should preserve those blisters in alcohol to show that I've really been of some use," she answered, happy in his approval.

"Sho! People are made for different uses. Some are fit only to shovel and dig. Others are here simply to decorate the world. Hard world. Hard work is for those who can't give society anything else, but beauty is its own excuse for being," he told her breezily.

"Now that's the first compliment you have given me," she pouted prettily. "I can get them in plenty back in the drawing-rooms where I am supposed to belong. We're to be real comrades here, and compliments are barred."

"I wasn't complimenting you," he maintained. "I was merely stating a principle of art."

"Then you mustn't make your principles of art personal, sir. But since you have, I'm going to refute the application of your principle and show how useful I've been. Now, sir, do you know what provisions we have outside of those you have just brought?"

He knew exactly, since he had investigated during the night. That they might possibly have to endure a siege of some weeks, he was quite well aware, and his first thought, after she had gone to sleep before the fire, had been to make inventory of such provisions as the prospector had left in his cabin. A knuckle of ham, part of a sack of flour, some navy beans, and some tea siftings at the bottom of a tin can; these constituted the contents of the larder which the miner had gone to replenish. But though the man knew he assumed ignorance, for he saw that she was bubbling over with the desire to show her forethought.

"Tell me," he begged of her, and after she had done so, he marveled aloud over her wisdom in thinking of it.

"Now tell me about your trip," she commanded, setting herself tailor fashion on the rug to listen.

"There isn't much to tell," he smiled "I should like to make an adventure of it, but I can't. I just went and came back."

"Oh, you just went and came back, did you?" she scoffed. "That won't do at all. I want to know all about it. Did you find the machine all right?"

"I found it where we left it, buried in four feet of snow. You needn't be afraid that anybody will run away with it for a day or two. The pantry was cached pretty deep itself, but I dug it out."

Her shy glance admired the sturdy lines of his powerful frame. "I am afraid it must have been a terrible task to get there through the blizzard."

"Oh, the blizzard is past. You never saw a finer, more bracing morning. It's a day for the gods," he laughed boyishly.

She could have conceived no Olympian more heroic than he, and certainly none with so compelling a vitality. "Such a warm, kind light in them!" she thought of the eyes others had found hard and calculating.

It was lucky that the lunch the automobilists had brought from Avalanche was ample and as yet untouched. The hotel waiter, who had attended to the packing of it, had fortunately been used to reckon with outdoor Montana appetites instead of cloyed New York ones. They unpacked the little hamper with much gaiety. Everything was frozen solid, and the wine had cracked its bottle.

"Shipped right through on our private refrigerator-car. That cold-storage chicken looks the finest that ever happened. What's this rolled up in tissue-paper? Deviled eggs and ham sandwiches AND caviar, not to speak of claret frappe. I'm certainly grateful to the gentleman finished in ebony who helped to provision us for this siege. He'll never know what a tip he missed by not being here to collect."

"Here's jelly, too, and cake," she said, exploring with him.

"Not to mention peaches and pears. Oh, this is luck of a special brand! I was expecting to put up at Starvation Camp. Now we may name it Point Plenty."

"Or Fort Salvation," she suggested shyly. "Because you brought me here to save my life."

She was such a child, in spite of her charming grown-up airs, that he played make-believe with a zest that surprised himself when he came to think of it. She elected him captain of Fort Salvation, with full power of life and death over the garrison, and he appointed her second in command. His first general order was to put the garrison on two meals a day.

She clapped her little hands, eyes sparkling with excitement. "Are we really snow-bound? Must we go on half-rations?"

"It is the part of wisdom, lieutenant," he answered, smiling at her enthusiasm. "We don't know how long this siege is going to last. If it should set in to snow, we may be here several days before the relief-party reaches us." But, though he spoke cheerfully, he was aware of sinister possibilities in the situation. "Several weeks" would have been nearer his real guess.

They ate breakfast at the shelf-table nailed in place underneath the western window. They made a picnic of it, and her spirits skipped upon the hilltops. For the first time she ate from tin plates, drank from a tin cup, and used a tin spoon the worse for rust. What mattered it to her that the teapot was grimy and the fryingpan black with soot! It was all part of the wonderful new vista that had suddenly opened before her gaze. She had awakened into life and already she was dimly realizing that many and varied experiences lay waiting for her in that untrodden path beyond her cloistered world.

A reconnaissance in the shed behind the house showed him no plethora of firewood. But here was ax, shovel, and saw, and he asked no more. First he shoveled out a path along the eaves of the house where she might walk in sentry fashion to take the deep breaths of clear sharp air he insisted upon. He made it wide enough so that her skirt would not sweep against the snow-bank, and trod down the trench till the footing was hard and solid. Then with ax and saw he climbed the hillside back of the house and set himself to get as much fuel as he could. The sky was still heavy with unshed snow, and he knew that with the coming of night the storm would be renewed.

Came noon, mid-afternoon, the early dusk of a mountain winter, and found him still hewing and sawing, still piling load after load in the shed. Now and again she came out and watched him, laughing at the figure he made as he would come plunging through the snow with his armful of fuel.

She did not know, as he did, the vital necessity of filling the lean-to before winter fell upon them in earnest and buried them deep with his frozen blanket, and she was a little piqued that he should spend the whole day away from her in such unsocial fashion.

"Let me help," she begged so often that he trod down a path, made boots for her out of torn gunny-sacks which he tied round her legs, and let her drag wood to the house on a pine branch which served for a sled. She wore her gauntlets to protect her tender hands, and thereafter was happy until, detecting signs of fatigue, he made her go into the house and rest.

As soon as she dared she was back again, making fun of him and the earnestness with which he worked.

"Robinson Crusoe" was one name she fastened upon him, and she was not satisfied till she had made him call her "Friday."

Twilight fell austere and sudden upon them with an immediate fall of temperature that found a thermometer in her blue face.

He recommended the house, but she was of a contrary mood.

"I don't want to," she announced debonairly.

In a stiff military attitude he gave raucous mandate from his throat.

"Commanding officer's orders, lieutenant."

"I think I'm going to mutiny," she informed him, with chin saucily in air.

This would not do at all. The chill wind sweeping down the canon was searching her insufficient clothing already. He picked her up in his arms and ran with her toward the house, setting her down in the trench outside the door. She caught her startled breath and looked at him in shy, dubious amazement.

"Really you " she was beginning when he cut her short.

"Commanding officer's orders, lieutenant," came briskly from lips that showed just a hint of a smile.

At once she clicked her heels together, saluted, and wheeled into the cabin.

From the grimy window she watched his broad-shouldered vigor, waving her hand whenever his face was turned her way. He worked like a Titan, reveling in the joy of physical labor, but it was long past dark before he finished and came striding to the hut.

They made a delightful evening of it, living in the land of Never Was. For one source of her charm lay in the gay, childlike whimsicality o her imagination. She believed in fairies and heroes with all her heart, which with her was an organ not located in her brain. The delicious gurgle of gaiety in her laugh was a new find to him in feminine attractions.

There had been many who thought the career of this pirate of industry beggared fiction, though, few had found his flinty personality a radiaton of romance. But this convent-nurtured child had made a discovery in men, one out of the rut of the tailor-made, convention-bound society youths to whom her experience for the most part had been limited. She delighted in his masterful strength, in the confidence of his careless dominance. She liked to see that look of power in his gray-blue eyes softened to the droll, half-tender, expression with which he played the game of make-believe. There were no to-morrows; to-day marked the limit of time for them. By tacit consent they lived only in the present, shutting out deliberately from their knowledge of each other, that past which was not common to both. Even their names were unknown to each other, and both of them were glad that it was so.

The long winter evening had fallen early, and they dined by candle-light, considering merrily how much they might with safety eat and yet leave enough for the to-morrows that lay before them. Afterward they sat before the fire, in the shadow and shine of the flickering logs, happy and content in each other's presence. She dreamed, and he, watching her, dreamed, too. The wild, sweet wonder of life surged through them, touching their squalid surroundings to the high mystery of things unreal.

The strangeness of it was that he was a man of large and not very creditable experience of women, yet her deep, limpid eyes, her sweet voice, the immature piquancy of her movements that was the expression of her, had stirred his imagination more potently than if he had been the veriest schoolboy nursing a downy lip. He could not keep his eyes from this slender, exquisite girl, so dainty and graceful in her mobile piquancy. Fire and passion were in his heart and soul, restraint and repression in his speech and manner. For the fire and passion in him were pure and clean as the winds that sweep the hills.

But for the girl—she was so little mistress of her heart that she had no prescience of the meaning of this sweet content that filled her. And the voices that should have warned her were silent, busy behind the purple hills with lies and love and laughter and tears.

CHAPTER 5

ENTER SIMON HARLEY

The prospector's house in which they had found refuge was perched on the mountainside just at one edge of the draw. Rough as the girl had thought it, there was a more pretentious appearance to it than might have been expected. The cabin was of hewn logs mortared with mud, and care had been taken to make it warm. The fireplace was a huge affair that ate fuel voraciously. It was built of stone, which had been gathered from the immediate hillside.

The prospect itself showed evidence of having been worked a good deal, and it was an easy guess for the man who now stood looking into the tunnel that it belonged to some one of the thousands of miners who spend half their time earning a grubstake, and the other half dissipating it upon some hole in the ground which they have duped themselves into believing is a mine.

From the tunnel his eye traveled up the face of the white mountain to the great snow-comb that yawned over the edge of the rock-rim far above. It had snowed again heavily all night, and now showed symptoms of a thaw. Not once nor twice, but a dozen times, the man's anxious gaze had swept up to that great overhanging bank. Snowslides ran every year in this section with heavy loss to life and property. Given a rising temperature and some wind, the comb above would gradually settle lower and lower, at last break off, plunge down the precipitous slope, bringing thousands of tons of rock and snow with it, and, perhaps, bury them in a Titanic grave of ice. There had been a good deal of timber cut from the shoulder of the mountain during the past summer, and this very greatly increased the danger. That there was a real peril the man looking at it did not attempt to deny to himself. It would be enough to deny it to her in case she should ever suspect.

He had hoped for cold weather, a freeze hard enough to crust the surface of the snow. Upon this he might have made shift somehow to get her to Yesler's ranch, eighteen miles away though it was, but he knew this would not be feasible with the snow in its present condition. It was not certain that he could make the ranch alone; encumbered with her, success would be a sheer impossibility. On the other hand, their provisions would not last long. The outlook was not a cheerful one, from whichever point of view he took it; yet there was one phase of it he could not regret. The factors which made the difficulties of the situation made also its delights. Though they were prisoners in this solitary untrodden caynon, the sentence was upon both of them. She could look to none other than he for aid; and, at least, the drifts which kept them in held others out.

Her voice at his shoulder startled him.

"Wherefore this long communion with nature, my captain?" she gaily asked. "Behold, my, lord's hot cakes are ready for the pan and his servant to wait upon him." She gave him a demure smiling little curtsy of mock deference.

Never had her distracting charm been more in evidence. He

had not seen her since they parted on the previous night. He had built for himself a cot in the woodshack, and had contrived a curtain that could be drawn in front of her bed in the living-room. Thus he could enter in the morning, light the fires, and start breakfast without disturbing her. She had dressed her hair, now in a different way, so that it fell in low waves back from the forehead and was bunched at the nape of her neck. The light swiftness of her dainty grace, the almost exaggerated carnation of the slightly parted lips, the glad eagerness that sparked her eyes, brought out effectively the picturesqueness of her beauty.

His grave eyes rested on her so long that a soft glow mantled her cheeks. Perhaps her words had been too free, though she had not meant them so. For the first time some thought of the conventions distressed her. Ought she to hold herself more in reserve toward him? Must she restrain her natural impulses to friendliness?

His eyes released her presently, but not before she read in them the feelings that had softened them as they gazed into hers. They mirrored his poignant pleasure at the delight of her sweet slenderness so close to him, his perilous joy at the intimacy fate had thrust upon them. Shyly her lids fell to the flushed cheeks.

"Breakfast is ready," she added self-consciously, her girlish innocence startled like a fawn of the forest at the hunter's approach

For whereas she had been blind now she saw in part. Some flash of clairvoyance had laid bare a glimpse of his heart and her own to her. Without misunderstanding the perfect respect for her which he felt, she knew the turbid banked emotions which this dammed. Her heart seemed to beat in her bosom like an imprisoned dove.

It was his voice, calm and resonant with strength, that brought her to earth again.

"And I am ready for it, lieutenant. Right about face. Forward—march!"

After breakfast they went out and tramped together the little path of hard-trodden snow in front of the house. She broached the prospect of a rescue or the chances of escape.

"We shall soon be out of food, and, anyhow, we can't stay here all winter," she suggested with a tremulous little laugh.

"You are naturally very tired of it already," he hazarded.

"It has been the experience of my life. I shall fence it off from all the days that have passed and all that are to come," she made answer vividly.

Their eyes met, but only for an instant.

"I am glad," he said quietly.

He began, then, to tell her what he must do, but at the first word of it she broke out in protest.

"No—no—no! We shall stay together. If you go I am going, too."

"I wish you could, but it is not possible. You could never get there. The snow is too soft and heavy for wading and not firm enough to bear your weight."

"But you will have to wade."

"I am stronger than you, lieutenant."

"I know, but—" She broke down and confessed her terror. "Would you leave me here—alone—with all this snow Oh, I couldn't stay—I couldn't."

"It's the only way," he said steadily. Every fiber in him rebelled at leaving her here to face peril alone, but his reason overrode the desire and rebellion that were hot within him. He must think first of her ultimate safety, and this lay in getting her away from here at the first chance.

Tears splashed down from the big eyes. "I didn't think you would leave me here alone. With you I don't mind it, but—Oh, I should die if I stayed alone."

"Only for twenty-four hours. Perhaps less. I shouldn't think of it if it weren't necessary."

"Take me with you. I am strong. You don't know how strong I am. I promise to keep up with you. Please!"

He shook his head. "I would take you with me if I could. You know that. But it's a man's fight. I shall have to stand up to it hour after hour till I reach Yesler's ranch. I shall get through, but it would not be possible for you to make it."

"And if you don't get through?"

He refused to consider that contingency. -"But I shall. You may look to see me back with help by this time to-morrow morning."

"I'm not afraid with you. But if you go away Oh, I can't stand it. You don't know—you don't know." She buried her face in her hands.

He had to swallow down his sympathy before he went on.

"Yes, I know. But you must be brave. You must think of every minute as being one nearer to the time of my return."

"You will think me a dreadful coward, and I am. But I can't help it. I AM afraid to stay alone. There's nothing in the world but mountains of snow. They are horrible—like death—except when you are here."

Her child eyes coaxed him to stay. The mad longing was in him to kiss the rosy little mouth with the queer alluring droop to its corners. It was a strange thing how, with that arched twist to her eyebrows and with that smile which came and went like sunshine in her eyes, she toppled his lifelong creed. The cardinal tenet of his faith had been a belief in strength. He had first been drawn to Virginia by reason of her pluck and her power. Yet this child's very weakness was her fountain of strength. She cried out with pain, and he counted it an asset of virtue in her. She acknowledged herself a coward, and his heart went out to her because of it. The battle assignments of life were not for the soft curves and shy winsomeness of this dainty lamb.

"You will be brave. I expect you to be brave, lieutenant." Words of love and comfort were crowding to his brain, but he would not let them out.

"How long will you be gone?" she sobbed.

"I may possibly get back before midnight, but you mustn't begin to expect me until to-morrow morning, perhaps not till to-morrow afternoon."

"Oh, I couldn't—I couldn't stay here at night alone. Don't go, please. I'll not get hungry, truly I won't, and to-morrow they will find us."

He rose, his face working. "I MUST go, child. It's the thing to do. I wish to Heaven it weren't. You must think of yourself as quite safe here. You ARE safe. Don't make it hard for me to go, dear."

"I AM a coward. But I can't help it. There is so much snow—and the mountains are so big." She tried valiantly to crush down her sobs. "But go. I'll—I'll not be afraid."

He buried her little hands in his two big ones and looked deep into her eyes. "Every minute of the time I am away from you I shall be with you in spirit. You'll not be alone any minute of the day or night. Whether you are awake or asleep I shall be with you."

"I'll try to remember that," she answered, smiling up at him but with a trembling lip.

She put him up some lunch while he made his simple preparations. To the end of the trench she walked with him, neither of them saying a word. The moment of parting had come.

She looked up at him with a crooked wavering little smile. She wanted to be brave, but she could not trust herself to say a word.

"Remember, dear. I am not leaving you. My body has gone on an errand. That is all."

Just now she found small comfort in this sophistry, but she did not tell him so.

"I—I'll remember." She gulped down a sob and still smiled through the mist that filmed her sight.

In his face she could see how much he was moved at her distress. Always a creature of impulse, one mastered her now, the need to let her weakness rest on his strength. Her arms slipped quickly round his neck and her head lay buried on his shoulder. He held her tight, eyes shining, the desire of her held in leash behind set teeth, the while sobs shook her soft round body in gusts.

"My lamb—my sweet precious lamb," she heard him murmur in anguish.

From some deep sex trait it comforted her that he suffered. With the mother instinct she began to regain control of herself that she might help him.

"It will not be for long," she assured him. "And every step of your way I shall pray for, your safety," she whispered.

He held her at arm's length while his gaze devoured her, then silently he wheeled away and plunged waist deep into the drifts. As long as he was in sight he saw her standing there, waving her handkerchief to him in encouragement. Her slight, dark figure, outlined against the snow, was the last thing his eyes fell upon before he turned a corner of the gulch and dropped downward toward the plains.

But when he was surely gone, after one fearful look at the white sea which encompassed her, the girl fled to the cabin, slammed the door after her, and flung herself on the bed to weep out her lonely terror in an ecstasy of tears. She had spent the first violence of her grief, and was sitting crouched on the rug before the open fire when the sound of a footstep, crunching the snow, startled her. The door opened, to let in the man who had just left her.

"You are back—already," she cried, her tear? stained face

lifted toward him.

"Yes," he smiled' from the doorway. "Come here, little partner."

And when she had obediently joined him her eye followed his finger up the mountain-trail to a bend round which men and horses were coming.

"It's a relief-party," he said, and caught up his field-glasses to look them over more certainly. Two men on horseback, leading a third animal, were breaking a way down the trail, black spots against the background of white. "I guess Fort Salvation's about to be relieved," he added grimly, following the party through the glasses.

She touched the back of his hand with a finger. "Are you glad?" she asked softly.

"No, by Heaven!" he cried, lowering his glasses swiftly.

As he looked into her eyes the blood rushed to his brain with a surge. Her face turned to his unconsciously, and their lips met.

"And I don't even know your name," she murmured.

"Waring Ridgway; and yours?"

"Aline Hope," she said absently. Then a hot Rush ran over the girlish face. "No, no, I had forgotten. I was married last week."

The gates of paradise, open for two days, clanged to on Ridgway. He stared out with unseeing eyes into the silent wastes of snow. The roaring in his ears and the mountainsides that churned before his eyes were reflections of the blizzard raging within him.

"I'll never forget—never," he heard her falter, and her voice was a thousand miles away.

From the storm within him he was aroused by a startled cry from the girl at his side. Her fascinated gaze was fixed on the summit of the ridge above them. There was a warning crackle. The overhanging comb snapped, slid slowly down, and broke off. With gathering momentum it descended, sweeping into its heart rocks, trees, and debris. A terrific roar filled the air as the great white cloud came tearing down like an express-train.

Ridgway caught her round the waist and flung the girl against the wall of the cabin, protecting her with his body. The avalanche was upon them, splitting great trees to kindling-wood in the fury of its rush. The concussion of the wind shattered every window to fragments, almost tore the cabin from its foundations. Only the extreme tail of the slide touched them, yet they were buried deep in flying snow.

He found no great difficulty in digging a way out, and when he lifted her to the surface she was conscious. Yet she was pale even to the lips and trembled like an aspen in the summer breeze, clinging to him for support helplessly.

His cheerful voice rang like a bugle to her shocked brain.

"It's all past. We're safe now, dear—quite safe."

The first of the trail-breakers had dismounted and was plowing his way hurriedly to the cabin, but neither of them saw him as he came up the slope.

William MacLeod Raine

"Are you sure?" She shuddered, her hands still in his. "Wasn't it awful? I thought—" Her sentence trailed out unfinished.

"Are you unhurt, Aline?" cried the newcomer. And when he saw she was, he added: "Praise ye the Lord. O give thanks unto the Lord; for He is good: for His mercy endureth forever. He saved them for His name's sake, that He might make His mighty power to be known."

At sound of the voice they turned and saw the man hurrying toward them. He was tall, gray, and seventy, of massive frame and gaunt, still straight and vigorous, with the hooked nose and piercing eyes of a hawk. At first glance he looked always the bird of prey, but at the next as invariably the wolf, an effect produced by the salient reaching jaw and the glint of white teeth bared for a lip smile. Just now he was touched to a rare emotion. His hands trembled and an expression of shaken thankfulness rested in his face.

Aline, still with Ridgway's strong arms about her, slowly came back to the inexorable facts of life.

"You—here?"

"As soon as we could get through—and thank God in time."

"I would have died, except for—" This brought her immediately to an introduction, and after she had quietly released herself the man who had saved her heard himself being formally presented: "Mr. Ridgway, I want you to meet my husband, Mr. Harley."

Ridgway turned to Simon Harley a face of hammered steel and bowed, putting his hands deliberately behind his back.

"I've been expecting you at Mesa, Mr. Harley," he said rigidly. "I'll be glad to have the pleasure of welcoming you there."

The great financier was wondering where he had heard the man's name before, but he only said gravely: "You have a claim on me I can never forget, Mr. Ridgway."

Scornfully the other disdained this proffer. "Not at all. You owe me nothing, Mr. Harley—absolutely nothing. What I have done I have done for her. It is between her and me."

At this moment the mind of Harley fitted the name Ridgway to its niche in his brain. So this was the audacious filibuster who had dared to fire on the trust flag, the man he had come West to ruin and to humble.

"I think you will have to include me, Mr. Ridgway," he said suavely. "What is done for my wife is done, also, for me."

William MacLeod Raine

CHAPTER 6

ON THE SNOW-TRAIL

Aline had passed into the house, moved by an instinct which shrank from publicity in the inevitable personal meeting between her and her husband. Now, Harley, with the cavalier nod of dismissal, which only a multimillionaire can afford, followed her and closed the door. A passionate rush of blood swept Ridgway's face. He saw red as he stood there with eyes burning into that door which had been shut in his face. The nails of his clenched fingers bit into his palms, and his muscles gathered themselves tensely. He had been cast aside, barred from the woman he loved by this septuagenarian, as carelessly as if he had no claim.

And it came home to him that now he had no claim, none before the law and society. They had walked in Arcadia where shepherds pipe. They had taken life for granted as do the creatures of the woods, forgetful of the edicts of a world that had seemed far and remote. But that world had obtruded itself and shattered their dream. In the person of Simon Harley it had shut the door which was to separate him and her. Hitherto he had taken from life what he had wanted, but already he was grappling with the blind fear of a fate for once too strong for him.

"Well, I'm damned if it isn't Waring Ridgway," called a mellow voice from across the gulch.

The man named turned, and gradually the set lines of his jaw relaxed.

"I didn't notice it was you, Sam. Better bring the horses across this side of that fringe of aspens."

The dismounted horseman followed directions and brought the floundering horses through, and after leaving them in the cleared place where Ridgway had cut his firewood he strolled leisurely forward to meet the mine-owner. He was a youngish man, broad of shoulder and slender of waist, a trifle bowed in the legs from much riding, but with an elastic sufficiency that promised him the man for an emergency, a pledge which his steady steel-blue eyes, with the humorous lines about the corners, served to make more valuable. His apparel suggested the careless efficiency of the cow-man, from the high-heeled boots into which were thrust his corduroys to the broad-brimmed white Stetson set on his sunreddened wavy hair. A man's man, one would vote him at first sight, and subsequent impressions would not contradict the first.

"Didn't know you were down in this neck of woods, Waring," he said pleasantly, as they shook hands.

An onlooker might have noticed that both of them gripped hands heartily and looked each other squarely in the eye.

"I came down on business and got caught in the blizzard on my way back. Came on her freezing in the machine and brought her here along with me. I had my eye on that slide. The snow up there didn't look good to me, and the grub was about out, anyhow, so I was heading for the C B Ranch when

I sighted you."

"Golden luck for her. I knew it was a chance in a million that she was still alive, but Harley wanted to take it. Say, that old fellow's made of steel wire. Two of my boys are plugging along a mile or two behind us, but he stayed right with the game to a finish—and him seventy-three, mind you, and a New Yorker at that. The old boy rides like he was born in a saddle," said Sam Yesler with enthusiasm.

"I never said he was a quitter," conceded Ridgway ungraciously.

"You're right he ain't. And say, but he's fond of his wife. Soon as he struck the ranch the old man butted out again into the blizzard to get her—slipped out before we knew it. The boys rounded him up wandering round the big pasture, and none too soon neither. All the time we had to keep herd on him to keep him from taking another whirl at it. He was like a crazy man to tackle it, though he must a-known it was suicide. Funny how a man takes a shine to a woman and thinks the sun rises and sets by her. Far, as I have been able to make out women are much of a sameness, though I ain't setting up for a judge. Like as not this woman don't care a hand's turn for him."

"Why should she? He bought her with his millions, I suppose. What right has an old man like that with one foot in the grave to pick out a child and marry her? I tell you, Sam, there's something ghastly about it."

"Oh, well, I reckon when she sold herself she knew what she was getting. It's about an even thing—six of one and half a dozen of the other. There must be something rotten about a woman who will do a thing of that sort."

"Wait till you've seen her before passing judgment. And after you have you'll apologize if you're a white man for thinking such a thing about her," the miner said hotly.

Yesler looked at his friend in amiable surprise. "I don't reckon we need to quarrel about Simon Harley's matrimonial affairs, do we?" he laughed.

"Not unless you want to say any harm of that lamb."

A glitter of mischief gleamed from the cattleman's eyes. "Meaning Harley, Waring?"

"You know who I mean. I tell you she's an angel from heaven, pure as the driven snow."

"And I tell you that I'll take your word for it without quarreling with you," was the goodhumored retort. "What's up, anyhow? I never saw you so touchy before. You're a regular pepper-box."

The rescuers had brought food with them, and the party ate lunch before starting back. The cow-punchers of the C B had now joined them, both of them, as well as their horses, very tired with the heavy travel.

"This here Marathon race business through three-foot snow ain't for invalids like me and Husky," one of them said cheerfully, with his mouth full of sandwich. "We're also rans, and don't even show for place."

Yet though two of them had, temporarily at least, been rescued from imminent danger, and success beyond their expectations had met the others, it was a silent party. A blanket of depression seemed to rest upon it, which the good stories of Yesler and the genial nonsense of his man, Chinn, were unable to lift. Three of them, at least, were brooding over what the morning had brought forth, and trying to realize what it might mean for them.

"We'd best be going, I expect," said Yesler at last. "We've got a right heavy bit of work cut out for us, and the horses are through feeding. We can't get started any too soon for me."

Ridgway nodded silently. He knew that the stockman was dubious, as he himself was, about being able to make the return trip in safety. The horses were tired; so, too, were the men who had broken the heavy trail for so many miles, with the exception of Sam himself, who seemed built of whipcord and elastic. They would be greatly encumbered by the woman, for she would certainly give out during the journey. The one point in their favor was that they could follow a trail which had already been trodden down.

Simon Harley helped his wife into the boy's saddle on the back of the animal they had led, but his inexperience had to give way to Yesler's skill in fitting the stirrups to the proper length for her feet. To Ridgway, who had held himself aloof during this preparation, the stockman now turned with a wave of his hand toward his horse

"You ride, Waring."

"No, I'm fresh."

"All right. We'll take turns."

Ridgway led the party across the gulch, following the trail that had been swept by the slide. The cowboys followed him, next came Harley, his wife, and in the rear the cattleman. They descended the draw, and presently dipped over rolling ground to the plain beyond. The procession plowed steadily forward mile after mile, the pomes floundering through drifts after the man ahead.

Chinn, who had watched him breasting the soft heavy blanket that lay on the ground so deep and hemmed them in, turned to his companion.

"On the way coming I told you, Husky, we had the best man in Montana at our head. We got that beat now to a fare-you-well. We got the two best in this party, by crickey."

"He's got the guts, all right, but there ain't nothing on two legs can keep it up much longer," replied the other. "If you want to know, I'm about all in myself."

"Here, too," grunted the other. "And so's the bronc."

It was not, however, until dusk was beginning to fall that the leader stopped. Yesler's voice brought him up short in his tracks.

"Hold on, Waring. The lady's down."

Ridgway strode back past the exhausted cowboys and Harley, the latter so beaten with fatigue that he could scarce cling to the pommel of his saddle.

"I saw it coming. She's been done for a long time, but she hung on like a thoroughbred," explained Yesler from the snow-bank where Aline had fallen.

He had her in his arms and was trying to get at a flask of whisky in his hip-pocket.

"All right. I'll take care of her, Sam. You go ahead with your horse and break trail. I don't like the way this wind is rising.

It's wiping out the path you made when you broke through. How far's the ranch now?"

"Close to five miles."

Both men had lowered their voices almost to a whisper.

"It's going to be a near thing, Sam. Your men are played out. Harley will never make it without help. From now on every mile will be worse than the last."

Yesler nodded quietly. "Some one has got to go ahead for help. That's the only way."

"It will have to be you, of course. You know the road best and can get back quickest. Better take her pony. It's the fittest."

The owner of the C B hesitated an instant before he answered. He was the last man in the world to desert a comrade that was down, but his common sense told him his friend had spoken wisely. The only chance for the party was to get help to it from the ranch.

"All right. If anybody plays out beside her try to keep him going. If it comes to a showdown leave him for me to pick up. Don't let him stop the whole outfit."

"Sure. Better leave me that bottle of whisky. So-long."

"You're going to ride, I reckon?"

"Yes. I'll have to."

"Get up on my horse and I'll give her to you. That's right Well, I'll see you later."

And with that the stockman was gone. For long they could see him, plunging slowly forward through the drifts, getting always smaller and smaller, till distance and the growing darkness swallowed him.

Presently the girl in Ridgway's arms opened her eyes.

"I heard what you and he said," she told him quietly.

"About what?" he smiled down into the white face that looked up into his.

"You know. About our danger. I'm not afraid, not the least little bit."

"You needn't be. We're coming through, all right. Sam will make it to the ranch. He's a man in a million."

"I don't mean that. I'm not afraid, anyway, whether we do or not."

"Why?" he asked, his heart beating wildly.

"I don't know, but I'm not," she murmured with drowsy content.

But he knew if she did not. Her fear had passed because he was there, holding her in his arms, fighting to the last ounce of power in him for her life. She felt he would never leave her, and that, if it came to the worst, she would pass from life with him close to her. Again he knew that wild exultant beat of blood no woman before this one had ever stirred in him.

Harley was the first to give up. He lurched forward and slipped from the saddle to the snow, and could not be cursed into rising. The man behind dismounted, put down his burden, and dragged the old man to his feet.

"Here! This won't do. You've got to stick it out."

"I can't. I've reached my limit." Then testily: "'Are not my days few? Cease then, and let me alone,'" he added wearily, with his everready tag of Scripture.

The instant the other's hold on him relaxed the old man sank back. Ridgway dragged him up and cuffed him like a troublesome child. He knew this was no time for reasoning.

"Are you going to lie down and quit, you old loafer? I tell you the ranch is only a mile or two. Here, get into the saddle."

By sheer strength the younger man hoisted him into the seat. He was very tired himself, but the vital sap of youth in him still ran strong in his blood. For a few yards farther they pushed on before Harley slid down again and his horse stopped.

Ridgway passed him by, guiding his bronco in a half-circle through the snow.

"I'll send back help for you," he promised.

"It will be too late, but save her—save her," the old man begged.

"I will," called back the other between set teeth.

Chinn was the next to drop out, and after him the one he called Husky. Both their horses had been abandoned a mile or two back, too exhausted to continue. Each of them Ridgway urged to stick to the trail and come on as fast as they could.

He knew the horse he was riding could not much longer keep going with the double weight, and when at length its strength gave out completely he went on afoot, carrying her in his arms as on that eventful night when he had saved her from the blizzard.

It was so the rescue-party found him, still staggering forward with her like a man in a sleep, flesh and blood and muscles all protestant against the cruelty of his indomitable will that urged them on in spite of themselves. In a dream he heard Yesler's cheery voice, gave up his burden to one of the rescuers, and found himself being lifted to a fresh horse. From this dream he awakened to find himself before the great fire of the living-room of the ranch-house, wakened from it only long enough to know that somebody was undressing him and helping him into bed.

Nature, with her instinct for renewing life, saw to it that Ridgway slept round the clock. He arose fit for anything. His body, hard as nails, suffered no reaction from the terrific strain he had put upon it, and he went down to his breakfast with an appetite ravenous for whatever good things Yesler's Chinese cook might have prepared for him.

He found his host already at work on a juicy steak.

"Mornin'," nodded that gentleman. "Hope you feel as good as you look."

"I'm all right, barring a little stiffness in my muscles. I'll feel good as the wheat when I've got outside of the twin steak to that one you have."

Yesler touched a bell, whereupon a soft-footed Oriental

appeared, turned almond eyes on his proprietor, took orders and padded silently back to his kingdom—the kitchen. Almost immediately he reappeared with a bowl of oatmeal and a pitcher of cream.

"Go to it, Waring."

His host waved him the freedom of the diningroom, and Ridgway fell to. Never before had food tasted so good. He had been too sleepy to cat last night, but now he made amends. The steak, the muffins, the coffee, were all beyond praise, and when he came to the buckwheat hot cakes, sandwiched with butter and drenched with real maple syrup, his satisfied soul rose up and called Hop Lee blessed. When he had finished, Sam capped the climax by shoving toward him his case of Havanas.

Ridgway's eyes glistened. "I haven't smoked for days," he explained, and after the smoke had begun to rise, he added: "Ask what you will, even to the half of my kingdom, it's yours."

"Or half of the Consolidated's," amended his friend with twinkling eyes.

"Even so, Sam," returned the other equably. "And now, tell me how you managed to round us all up safely."

"You've heard, then, that we got the whole party in time?"

"Yes, I've been talking with one of your enthusiastic riders that went out with you after us. He's been flimflammed into believing you the greatest man in the United States. Tell me how you do it."

"Nick's a good boy, but I reckon he didn't tell you quite

all that."

"Didn't he? You should have heard him reel off your praises by the yard. I got the whole story of how you headed the relief-party after you had reached the ranch more dead than alive."

"Then, if you've got it, I don't need to tell you. I WAS a bit worried about the old man. He was pretty far gone when we reached him, but he pulled through all right. He's still sleeping like a top."

"Is he?" His guest's hard gaze came round to meet his. "And the lady? Do you know how she stood it?"

"My sister says she was pretty badly played out, but all she needs is rest. Nell put her in her own bed, and she, too, has been doing nothing but sleep."

Ridgway smoked out his cigar in silence then tossed it into the fireplace as he rose briskly.

"I want to talk to Mesa over the phone, Sam."

"Can't do it. The wires are down. This storm played the deuce with them."

"The devil! I'll have to get through myself then."

"Forget business for a day or two, Waring, and take it easy up here," counseled his host.

"Can't do it. I have to make arrangements to welcome Simon Harley to Mesa. The truth is, Sam, that there are several things that won't wait. I've got to frame them up my way. Can you get me through to the railroad in time to catch the Limited?"

"I think so. The road has been traveled for two or three days. If you really must go. I hate to have you streak off like this."

"I'd like to stay, Sam, but I can't. For one thing, there's that senatorial fight coming on. Now that Harley's on the ground in person, I'll have to look after my fences pretty close. He's a good fighter, and he'll be out to win."

"After what you've done for him. Don't you think that will make a difference, Waring?"

His friend laughed without mirth. "What have I done for him? I left him in the snow to die, and while a good many thousand other people would bless me for it, probably he has a different point of view."

"I was thinking of what you did for his wife."

"You've said it exactly. I did it for her, not for him. I'll accept nothing from Harley on that account. He is outside of the friendship between her and me, and he can't jimmy his way in."

Yesler shrugged his shoulders. " All right. I'll order a rig hitched for you and drive you over myself. I want to talk over this senatorial fight anyhow. The way things look now it's going to be the rottenest session of the legislature we've ever had. Sometimes I'm sick of being mixed up in the thing, but I got myself elected to help straighten out things, and I'm certainly going to try."

"That's right, Sam. With a few good fighters like you we can win out. Anything to beat the Consolidated."

"Anything to keep our politics decent," corrected the other. "I've got nothing against the Consolidated, but I won't lie down and let it or any other private concern hog-tie this State—not if I can help it, anyhow."

Behind wary eyes Ridgway studied him. He was wondering how far this man would go as his tool. Sam Yesler held a unique position in the State. His influence was commanding among the sturdy old-time population represented by the non-mining interests of the smaller towns and open plains. He must be won at all hazards to lend it in the impending fight against Harley. The mine-owner knew that no thought of personal gain would move him. He must be made to feel that it was for the good of the State that the Consolidated be routed. Ridgway resolved to make him see it that way.

William MacLeod Raine

CHAPTER 7

BACK FROM ARCADIA

The president of the Mesa Ore-producing Company stepped from the parlor-car of the Limited at the hour when all wise people are taking life easy after a good dinner. He did not, however, drive to his club, but took a cab straight for his rooms, where he had telegraphed Eaton to meet him with the general superintendent of all his properties and his private secretary, Smythe. For nearly a week his finger had been off the pulse of the situation, and he wanted to get in touch again as soon as possible. For in a struggle as tense as the one between him and the trust, a hundred vital things might have happened in that time. He might be coming back to catastrophe and ruin, brought about while he had been a prisoner to love in that snow-bound cabin.

Prisoner to love he had been and still was, but the business men who met him at his rooms, fellow adventurers in the forlorn hope he had hitherto led with such signal success, could have read nothing of this in the marble, chiseled face of their sagacious general, so indomitable of attack and insatiate of success. His steel-hard eyes gave no hint of the Arcadia they had inhabited so eagerly a short twenty-four hours before. The intoxicating madness he had known was chained deep within him. Once more he had a grip on himself; was sheathed in a cannonproof plate armor of selfishness. No more magic nights of starshine, breathing fire and dew; no more lifted moments of exaltation stinging him to a pulsating wonder at life's wild delight. He was again the inexorable driver of men, with no pity for their weaknesses any more than for his own.

The men whom he found waiting for him at his rooms were all young Westerners picked out by him because he thought them courageous, unscrupulous and loyal. Like him, they were privateers in the seas of commerce, and sailed under no flag except the one of insurrection he had floated. But all of them, though they were associated with him and hoped to ride to fortune on the wave that carried him there, recognized themselves as subordinates in the enterprises he undertook. They were merely heads of departments, and they took orders like trusted clerks with whom the owner sometimes unbends and advises.

Now he heard their reports, asked an occasional searching question, and swiftly gave decisions of far-reaching import. It was past midnight before he had finished with them, and instead of retiring for the sleep he might have been expected to need, he spent the rest of the night inspecting the actual workings of the properties he had not seen for six days. Hour after hour he passed examining the developments, sometimes in the breasts of the workings and again consulting with engineers and foremen in charge. Light was breaking in the sky before he stepped from the cage of the Jack Pot and boarded a street-car for his rooms. Cornishmen and Hungarians and Americans, going with their dinner-buckets to work, met him and received each a nod or a word of greeting from this splendidly built young Hermes in miners' slops, who was to many of them, in their fancy, a deliverer from the slavery which the Consolidated was ready to force upon them.

William MacLeod Raine

Once at his rooms, Ridgway took a cold bath, dressed carefully, breakfasted, and was ready to plunge into the mass of work which had accumulated during his absence at the mining camp of Alpine and the subsequent period while he was snowbound. These his keen, practical mind grasped and disposed of in crisp sentences. To his private secretary he rapped out order sharply and decisively.

"Phone Ballard and Dalton I want to see them at once. Tell Murphy I won't talk with him. What I said before I left was final. Write Cadwallader we can't do business on the terms he proposes, but add that I'm willing to continue his Mary Kinney lease. Dictate a letter to Riley's lawyer, telling him I can't afford to put a premium on incompetence and negligence; that if his client was injured in the Jack Pot explosion, he has nobody but himself to blame for it. Otherwise, of course, I should be glad to pension him. Let me see the letter before you send it. I don't want anything said that will offend the union. Have two tons of good coal sent up to Riley's house, and notify his grocer that all bills for the next three months may be charged to me. And, Smythe, ask Mr. Eaton to step this way."

Stephen Eaton, an alert, clear-eyed young fellow who served as fidus Achates to Ridgway, and was the secretary and treasurer of the Mesa Ore-producing Company, took the seat Smythe had vacated. He was good-looking, after a boyish, undistinguished fashion, but one disposed to be critical might have voted the chin not quite definite enough. He had been a clerk of the Consolidated, working for one hundred dollars a month, when Ridgway picked him out and set his feet in the way of fortune. He had done this out of personal liking, and, in return, the subordinate was frankly devoted to his chief.

"Steve, my opinion is that Alpine is a false alarm. Unless I guess wrong, it is merely a surface proposition and low-grade at that."

"Miller says—"

"Yes, I know what Miller says. He's wrong. I don't care if he is the biggest copper expert in the country."

"Then you won't invest?"

"I have invested—bought the whole outfit, lock, stock and barrel."

"But why? What do you want with it if the property is no good?" asked Eaton in surprise.

Ridgway laughed shortly. "I don't want it, but the Consolidated does. Two of their experts were up at Alpine last week, and both of them reported favorably. I've let it leak out to their lawyer, O'Malley, that Miller thought well of it; in fact, I arranged to let one of their spies steal a copy of his report to us."

"But when they know you have bought it "

"They won't know till too late. I bought through a dummy. It seemed a pity not to let then have the property since they wanted it so badly, so this morning he sold out for me to the Consolidated at a profit of a hundred and fifty thousand."

Eaton grinned appreciatively. It was in startling finesse of this sort his chief excelled, and Stephen was always ready with applause.

"I notice that Hobart slipped out of town last night. That is where he must have been going. He'll be sick when he learns how you did him."

Ridgway permitted himself an answering smile. "I suppose it will irritate him a trifle, but that can't be helped. I needed that money to get clear on that last payment for the Sherman Bell."

"Yes, I was worried about that. Notes have been piling up against us that must be met. There's the Ransom note, too. It's for a hundred thousand."

"He'll extend it," said the chief confidently.

"He told me he would have to have his money when it came due. I've noticed he has been pretty close to Mott lately. I expect he has an arrangement with the Consolidated to push us."

"I'm watching him, Steve. Don't worry about that. He did arrange to sell the note to Mott, but I stopped that little game."

"How?"

"For a year I've had all the evidence of that big government timber steal of his in a safety-deposit vault. Before he sold, I had a few words with him. He changed his mind and decided he preferred to hold the notes. More, he is willing to let us have another hundred thousand if we have to have it."

Eaton's delight bubbled out of him in boyish laughter. "You're a wonder, Waring. There's nobody like you. Can't any of them touch you—not Harley himself, by Jove."

"We'll have a chance to find that out soon, Steve."

"Yes, they say he's coming out in person to run the fight against you. I hope not."

"It isn't a matter of hoping any longer. He's here," calmly announced his leader.

"Here! On the ground?"

"Yes."

"But—he can't be here without us knowing it."

"I'm telling you that I do know it."

"Have you seen him yourself?" demanded the treasurer incredulously.

"Seen him, talked with him, cursed him and cuffed him," announced Ridgway with a reminiscent gleam in his eye.

"Er—what's that you say?" gasped the astounded Eaton.

"Merely that I have already met Simon Harley."

"But you said—"

"—that I had cursed and cuffed him. That's all right. I have."

The president of the Mesa Ore-producing Company leaned back with his thumbs in the armholes of his fancy waistcoat and smiled debonairly at his associate's perplexed amazement.

"Did you say—CUFFED him?"

"That's what I meant to say. I roughed him around quite a bit—manhandled him in general. But all FOR HIS GOOD, you know."

"For his good?" Eaton's dazed brain tried to conceive the

William MacLeod Raine

situation of a billionaire being mauled for his good, and gave it up in despair. If Steve Eaton worshipped anything, it was wealth. He was a born sycophant, and it was partly because his naive unstinted admiration had contributed to satisfy his chief's vanity that the latter had made of him a confidant. Now he sat dumb before the lese-majeste of laying forcible hands upon the richest man in the world.

"But, of course, you're only joking," he finally decided.

"You haven't been back twelve hours. Where COULD you have seen him?,"

"Nevertheless I have met him and been properly introduced by his wife."

"His wife?"

"Yes, I picked her out of a snow-drift."

"Is this a riddle?"

"If it is, I don't know the answer, Steve. But it is a true one, anyhow, not made to order merely to astonish you."

"True that you picked Simon Harley's wife out of a snow-drift and kicked him around?"

"I didn't say kicked, did I?" inquired the other, judicially. "But I rather think I did knee him some."

"Of course, I read all about his marriage two weeks ago to Miss Aline Hope. Did he bring her out here with him for the honeymoon?"

"If he did, I euchred him out of it. She spent it with me alone in a miner's cabin," the other cried, malevolence riding triumph on his face.

"Whenever you're ready to explain," suggested Eaton helplessly. "You've piled up too many miracles for me even to begin guessing them."

"You know I was snow-bound, but you did not know my only companion was this Aline Hope you speak of. I found her in the blizzard, and took her to an empty cabin near. She and her husband were motoring from Avalanche to Mesa, and the machine had broken down. Harley had gone for help and left her there alone when the blizzard came up. Three days later Sam Yesler and the old man broke trail through from the C B Ranch and rescued us."

It was so strange a story that it came home to Eaton piecemeal.

"Three days—alone with Harley's wife—and he rescued you himself."

"He didn't rescue me any. I could have broken through any time I wanted to leave her. On the way back his strength gave out, and that was when I roughed him. I tried to bullyrag him into keeping on, but it was no go. I left him there, and Sam went back after him with a relief-party."

"You left him! With his wife?"

"No!" cried Ridgway. "Do I look like a man to desert a woman on a snow-trail? I took her with me."

"Oh!" There was a significant silence before Eaton asked the question in his mind. "I've seen her pictures in the papers. Does she look like them?"

His chief knew what was behind the question, and he knew, too, that Eaton might be taken to represent public opinion. The world would cast an eye of review over his varied and discreditable record with women. It would imagine the story of those three days of enforced confinement together, and it would look to the woman in the case for an answer to its suspicions. That she was young, lovely, and yet had sold herself to an old man for his millions, would go far in itself to condemn her; and he was aware that there were many who would accept her very childish innocence as the sophistication of an artist.

Waring Ridgway put his arms akimbo on the table and leaned across with his steady eyes fastened on his friend.

"Steve, I'm going to answer that question. I haven't seen any pictures of her in the papers, but if they show a face as pure and true as the face of God himself then they are like her. You know me. I've got no apologies or explanations to make for the life I've led. That's my business. But you're my friend, and I tell you I would rather be hacked in pieces by Apaches than soil that child's white soul by a single unclean breath. There mustn't be any talk. Do you understand? Keep the story out of the newspapers. Don't let any of our people gossip about it. I have told you because I want you to know the truth. If any one should speak lightly about this thing stop him at once. This is the one point on which Simon Harley and I will pull together.

Any man who joins that child's name with mine loosely will have to leave this camp—and suddenly."

"It won't be the men—it will be the women that will talk."

"Then garble the story. Change that three days to three hours, Steve. Anything to stop their foul-clacking tongues!"

"Oh, well! I dare say the story won't get out at all, but if it does I'll see the gossips get the right version. I suppose Sam Yesler will back it up."

"Of course. He's a white man. And I don't need to tell you that I'll be a whole lot obliged to you, Stevie."

"That's all right. Sometimes I'm a white man, too, Waring," laughed Steve. Ridgway circled the table and put a hand on the younger man's shoulder affectionately. Steve Eaton was the one of all his associates for whom he had the closest personal feeling.

"I don't need to be told that, old pal," he said quietly.

CHAPTER 8

THE HONORABLE THOMAS B. PELTON

It was next morning that Steve came into Ridgway's offices with a copy of the Rocky Mountain Herald in his hands. As soon as the president of the Mesa Ore-producing Company was through talking with Dalton, the superintendent of the Taurus, about the best means of getting to the cage a quantity of ore he was looting from the Consolidated property adjoining, the treasurer plumped out with his news.

"Seen to-day's paper, Waring? It smokes out Pelton to a finish. They've moled out some facts we can't get away from."

Ridgway glanced rapidly over the paper. "We'll have to drop Pelton and find another candidate for the Senate. Sorry, but it can't be helped. They've got his record down too fine. That affidavit from Quinton puts an end to his chances."

"He'll kick like a bay steer."

"His own fault for not covering his tracks better. This exposure doesn't help us any at best. If we still tried to carry Pelton, we should last about as long as a snowball in hell."

"Shall I send for him?"

"No. He'll be here as quick as he can cover the ground. Have him shown in as soon as he comes. And Steve—did Harley arrive on the eight-thirty this morning?"

"Yes. He is putting up at the Mesa House. He reserved an entire floor by wire, so that he has bed-rooms, dining-rooms, parlors, reception-halls and private offices all together. The place is policed thoroughly, and nobody can get up without an order."

"I haven't been thinking of going up and shooting him, even though it would be a blessing to the country," laughed his chief.

"No, but it is possible somebody else might. This town is full of ignorant foreigners who would hardly think twice of it. If he had asked my advice, it would have been to stay away from Mesa."

"He wouldn't have taken it," returned Ridgway carelessly. "Whatever else is true about him, Simon Harley isn't a coward. He would have told you that not a sparrow falls to the ground without the permission of the distorted God he worships, and he would have come on the next train."

"Well, it isn't my funeral," contributed Steve airily.

"All the same I'm going to pass his police patrols and pay a visit to the third floor of the Mesa House."

"You are going to compromise with him?" cried Eaton swiftly.

"Compromise nothing, I'm going to pay a formal social call

on Mrs. Harley, and respectfully hope that she has suffered no ill effects from her exposure to the cold."

Eaton made no comment, unless to whistle gently were one.

"You think it isn't wise "

"Well, is it?" asked Steve.

"I think so. We'll scotch the lying tongue of rumor by a strict observance of the conventions. Madam Grundy is padlocked when we reduce the situation to the absurdity of the common place."

"Perhaps you are right, if it doesn't become too common commonplace."

"I think we may trust Simon Harley to see to that," answered his chief with a grim smile "Obviously our social relations aren't likely to be very intimate. Now it's 'Just before the battle mother,' but once the big guns begin to boor we'll neither of us be in the mood for functions social."

"You've established a sort of claim on him. It wouldn't surprise me if he would meet you halfway in settling the trouble between you," said Eaton thoughtfully.

"I expect he would," agreed Ridgway indifferently as he lit a cigar.

"Well, then?"

"The trouble is that I won't meet him halfway. I can't afford to be reasonable, Steve. Just suppose for an instant that I had been reasonable five years ago when this fight began. They would have bought me out for a miserable pittance of a hundred and fifty thousand or so. That would have been a reasonable figure then. You might put it now at five or six millions, and that would be about right. I don't want their money. I want power, and I'd rather fight for it than not. Besides, I mean to make what I have already wrung from them a lever for getting more. I'm going to show Harley that he has met a man at last he can't either freeze out or bully out. I'm going to let him and his bunch know I'm on earth and here to stay; that I can beat them at their own game to a finish."

"Did it ever occur to you, Waring, that it might pay to make this a limited round contest? You've won on points up to date by a mile, but in a finish fight endurance counts. Money is the same as endurance here, and that's where they are long."

Eaton made this suggestion diffidently, for though he was a stockholder and official of the Mesa Ore-producing Company, he was not used to offering its head unasked advice. The latter, however, took it without a trace of resentment.

"Glad of it, my boy. There's no credit in beating a cripple."

To this jaunty retort Eaton had found no answer when Smythe opened the door to announce the arrival of the Honorable Thomas B. Pelton, very anxious for an immediate interview with Mr. Ridgway.

"Show him in," nodded the president, adding in an aside: "You better stay, Steve."

Pelton was a rotund oracular individual in silk hat and a Prince Albert coat of broadcloth. He regarded himself solemnly as a statesman because he had served two inconspicuous terms in the House at Washington. He was fond of proclaiming himself a Southern gentleman, part of which statement was unnecessary and part untrue. Like many from his section, he had a decided penchant for politics.

"Have you seen the infamous libel in that scurrilous sheet of the gutters the Herald?" he demanded immediately of Ridgway.

"Which libel? They don't usually stop at one, colonel."

"The one, seh, which slanders my honorable name; which has the scoundrelly audacity to charge me with introducing the mining extension bill for venal reasons, seh."

"Oh! Yes, I've seen that. Rather an unfortunate story to come out just now."

"I shall force a retraction, seh, or I shall demand the satisfaction due a Southern gentleman.

"Yes, I would, colonel," replied Ridgway, secretly amused at the vain threats of this bag of wind which had been punctured.

"It's a vile calumny, an audacious and villainous lie."

"What part of it? I've just glanced over it, but the part I read seems to be true. That's the trouble with it. If it were a lie you could explode it."

"I shall deny it over my signature."

"Of course. The trouble will be to get people to believe your denial with Quinton's affidavit staring them in the face. It seems they have got hold of a letter, too, that you wrote. Deny it, of course, then lie low and give the public time to forget it."

"Do you mean that I should withdraw from the senatorial race?"

"That's entirely as you please, colonel, but I'm afraid you'll find your support will slip away from you."

"Do you mean that YOU won't support me, seh?"

Ridgway locked his hands behind his head and leaned back in his chair. "We've got to face facts, colonel. In the light of this exposure you can't be elected."

"But I tell you, by Gad, seh, that I mean to deny it."

"Certainly. I should in your place," agreed the mine-owner coolly. "The question is, how many people are going to believe you?"

Tiny sweat-beads stood on the forehead of the Arkansan. His manner was becoming more and more threatening. "You pledged me your support. Are you going to throw me down, seh?"

"You have thrown yourself down, Pelton. Is it my fault you bungled the thing and left evidence against you? Am I to blame because you wrote incriminating letters?"

"Whatever I did was done for you," retorted the cornered man desperately.

"I beg your pardon. It was done for what was in it for you. The arrangement between us was purely a business one."

The coolness of his even voice maddened the harassed Pelton.

"So I'm to get burnt drawing your chestnuts out of the fire, am I? You're going to stand back and let my career be sacrificed, are you? By Gad, seh, I'll show you whether I'll be your catspaw," screamed the congressman.

"Use your common sense, Pelton, and don't shriek like a fish-wife," ordered Ridgway sharply. "No sane man floats a leaky ship. Go to drydock and patch up your reputation, and in a few years you'll come out as good as new."

All his unprincipled life Pelton had compromised with honor to gain the coveted goal he now saw slipping from him. A kind of madness of despair surged up in him. He took a step threateningly toward the seated man, his hand slipping back under his coat-tails toward his hip pocket. Acridly his high voice rang out.

"As a Southern gentleman, seh, I refuse to tolerate the imputations you cast upon me. I demand an apology here and now, seh."

Ridgway was on his feet and across the room like a flash.

"Don't try to bully ME, you false alarm. Call yourself a Southern gentleman! You're a shallow scurvy impostor. No more like the real article than a buzzard is like an eagle. Take your hand from under that coat or I'll break every bone in your flabby body."

Flabby was the word, morally no less than physically. Pelton quailed under that gaze which bored into him like a gimlet. The ebbing color in his face showed he could summon no reserve of courage sufficient to meet it. Slowly his empty hand came forth.

"Don't get excited, Mr. Ridgway. You have mistaken my

purpose, seh. I had no intention of drawing," he stammered with a pitiable attempt at dignity.

"Liar," retorted his merciless foe, crowding him toward the door.

"I don't care to have anything more to do with you. Our relations are at an end, seh," quavered Pelton as he vanished into the outer once and beat a hasty retreat to the elevator.

Ridgway returned to his chair, laughing ruefully. "I couldn't help it, Steve. He would have it. I suppose I've made one more enemy."

"A nasty one, too. He'll stick at nothing to get even."

"We'll draw his fangs while there is still time. Get a good story in the Sun to the effect that I quarreled with him as soon as I discovered his connection with this mining extension bill graft. Have it in this afternoon's edition, Steve. Better get Brayton to write it."

Steve nodded. "That's a good idea. We may make capital out of it after all. I'll have an editorial in, too. 'We love him for the enemies he has made.' How would that do for a heading?"

"Good. And now we'll have to look around for a candidate to put against Mott. I'm hanged if I know where we'll find one."

Eaton had an inspiration.

"I do?"

"One that will run well, popular enough to catch the public fancy?"

"Yes."

"Who, then?"

"Waring Ridgway."

The owner of the name stared at his lieutenant in astonishment, but slowly the fascination o the idea sank in.

"By Jove! Why not?"

CHAPTER 9

AN EVENING CALL

"Says you're to come right up, Mr. Ridgway," the bell-hop reported, and after he had pocketed his tip, went sliding off across the polished floor to answer another call.

The president of the Mesa Ore-producing Company turned with a good-humored smile to the chief clerk.

"You overwork your boys, Johnson. I wasn't through with that one. I'll have to ask you to send another up to show me the Harley suite."

They passed muster under the eye of the chief detective, and, after the bell-boy had rung, were admitted to the private parlor where Simon Harley lay stretched on a lounge with his wife beside him. She had been reading, evidently aloud and when her visitor was announced rose with her finger still keeping the place in the closed book.

The gaze she turned on him was of surprise, almost of alarm, so that the man on the threshold knew he was not expected.

"You received my card?" he asked quickly.

William MacLeod Raine

"No. Did you send one?" Then, with a little gesture of half-laughing irritation: "It must have gone to Mr. Harvey again. He is Mr. Harley's private secretary, and ever since we arrived it has been a comedy of errors. The hotel force refuses to differentiate."

"I must ask you to accept my regrets for an unintentional intrusion, Mrs. Harley. When I was told to come up, I could not guess that my card had gone amiss."

The great financier had got to his feet and now came forward with extended hand.

"Nevertheless we are glad to see you, Mr. Ridgway, and to get the opportunity to express our thanks for all that you have done for us."

The cool fingers of the younger man touched his lightly before they met those of his wife.

"Yes, we are very glad, indeed, to see you, Mr. Ridgway," she added to her husband's welcome.

"I could not feel quite easy in my mind without hearing from your own lips that you are none the worse for the adventures you have suffered," their visitor explained after they had found seats.

"Thanks to you, my wife is quite herself again, Mr. Ridgway," Harley announced from the davenport. "Thanks also to God, who so mercifully shelters us beneath the shadow of His wing."

But her caller preferred to force from Aline's own lips this affidavit of health. Even his audacity could not ignore his host entirely, but it gave him the least consideration possible.

To the question which still rested in his eyes the girl-wife answered shyly.

"Indeed, I am perfectly well. I have done nothing but sleep to-day and yesterday. Miss Yesler was very good to me. I do not know how I can repay the great kindness of so many friends," she said with a swift descent of fluttering lashes to the soft cheeks upon which a faint color began to glow.

"Perhaps they find payment for the service in doing it for you," he suggested.

"Yet, I shall take care not to forget it," Harley said pointedly.

"Indeed!" Ridgway put it with polite insolence, the hostility in his face scarcely veiled.

"It has pleased Providence to multiply my portion so abundantly that I can reward those well who serve me."

"At how much do you estimate Mrs. Harley's life?" his rival asked with quiet impudence.

In the course of the past two days Aline had made the discovery that her husband and her rescuer were at swords drawn in a business way. This had greatly distressed her, and in her innocence she had resolved to bring them together. How could her inexperience know that she might as well have tried to induce the lion and the lamb to lie down together peaceably? Now she tried timidly to drift the conversation from the awkwardness into which Harley's suggestion of a reward and his opponent's curt retort had blundered it.

"I hope you did not find upon your return that your business was disarranged so much as you feared it might be by your absence."

"I found my affairs in very good condition," Ridgway smiled. "But I am glad to be back in time to welcome to Mesa you—and Mr. Harley."

"It seems so strange a place," the girl ventured, with a hesitation that showed her anxiety not to offend his local pride. "You see I never before was in a place where there was no grass and nothing green in sight. And to-night, when I looked out of the window and saw streams of red-hot fire running down hills, I thought of Paradise Lost and Dante. I suppose it doesn't seem at all uncanny to you?"

"At night sometimes I still get that feeling, but I have to cultivate it a bit," he confessed. "My sober second thought insists that those molten rivers are merely business, refuse disgorged as lava from the great smelters."

"I looked for the sun to-day through the pall of sulphur smoke that hangs so heavy over the town, but instead I saw a London gas-lamp hanging in the heavens. Is it always so bad?"

"Not when the drift of the wind is right. In fact, a day like this is quite unusual."

"I'm glad of that. I feel more cheerful in the sunshine. I know that's a bit of the child still left in me. Mr. Harley takes all days alike."

The Wall Street operator was in slippers and house-jacket. His wife, too, was dressed comfortably in some soft clinging stuff. Their visitor saw that they had disposed themselves for a quiet uninterrupted evening by the fireside. The domesticity of it all stirred the envy in him. He did not want her to be contented and at peace with his enemy. Something deeper than his vanity cried out in protest against it.

She was still making talk against the gloom of the sulphur fog which seemed to have crept into the spirit of the room.

"We were reading before you came in, Mr. Ridgway. I suppose you read a good deal. Mr. Harley likes to have me read aloud to him when he is tired."

An impulse came upon Ridgway to hear her, some such impulse as makes a man bite on sore tooth even though he knows he must pay later for it.

"Will you not go on with your reading? I should like to hear it. I really should."

She was a little taken aback, but she looked inquiringly at her husband, who bowed silently.

"I was just beginning the fifty-ninth psalm. We have been reading the book through. Mr. Harley finds great comfort in it," she explained.

Her eyes fell to the printed page and her clear, sweet voice took up the ancient tale of vengeance

"Deliver me from mine enemies, O my God: defend me from them that rise up against me. Deliver me from the workers of iniquity, and save me from bloody men.

"For, lo, they lie in wait for my soul: the mighty are gathered against me; not for my transgression, nor for my sin, O Lord. They run and prepare themselves without my fault: awake to help me, and behold.

"Thou, therefore, O Lord God of Hosts, the God of Israel, awake to visit all the heathen: be not merciful to any wicked transgressors. Selah."

Ridgway glanced across in surprise at the strong old man lying on the lounge. His hands were locked in front of him, and his gaze rested peacefully on the fair face of the child reading. His foe's mind swept up the insatiable cruel years that lay behind this man, and he marveled that with such a past he could still hold fast to that simple faith of David. He wondered whether this ruthless spoiler went back to the Old Testament for the justification of his life, or whether his credo had given the impulse to his career. One thing he no longer doubted: Simon Harley believed his Bible implicitly and literally, and not only the New Testament.

"For the sin of their mouth and the words of their lips even be taken in their pride: and for cursing and lying which they speak.

"Consume them in wrath, consume them, that they may not be: and let them know that God ruleth in Jacob unto the ends of the earth."

The fresh young girlish voice died away into silence. Harley, apparently deep in meditation, gazed at the ceiling. His guest felt a surge of derision at this man who thought he had a compact with God to rule the world for his benefit.

"I am sure Mr. Harley must enjoy the Psalms a great deal," he said ironically, but it was in simple faith the young wife answered eagerly:

"He does. He finds so much in them that is applicable to life."

"I can see how he might," agreed the young man.

"Few people take their religion so closely into their every-day lives as he does," she replied in a low voice, seeing that her husband was lost in thought.

"I am sure you are right."

"He is very greatly misunderstood, Mr. Ridgway. I am sure if people knew how good he is—But how can they know when the newspapers are so full of falsehoods about him? And the magazines are as bad, he says. It seems to be the fashion to rake up bitter things to say about prominent business men. You must have noticed it."

"Yes. I believe I have noticed that," he answered with a grim little laugh.

"Don't you think it could be explained to these writers? They can't WANT to distort the truth. It must be they don't know."

"You must not take the muckrakers too seriously. They make a living roasting us. A good deal of what they say is true in a way. Personally, I don't object to it much. It's a part of the penalty of being successful. That's how I look at it."

"Do they say bad things about you, too?" she asked in open-eyed surprise.

"Occasionally," he smiled. "When they think I'm important enough."

"I don't see how they can," he heard her murmur to herself.

"Oh, most of what they say is true."

"Then I know it can't be very bad," she made haste to answer.

"You had better read it and see."

"I don't understand business at all," she said

"But—sometimes it almost frightens me. Business isn't really like war, is it?"

"A good deal like it. But that need not frighten you. All life is a battle—sometimes, at least. Success implies fighting."

"And does that in turn imply tragedy—for the loser?"

"Not if one is a good loser. We lose and make another start."

"But if success is a battle, it must be gained at the expense of another."

"Sometimes. But you must look at it in a big way." The secretary of the trust magnate had come in and was in low-toned conversation with him. The visitor led her to the nearest window and drew back the curtains so that they looked down on the lusty life of the turbid young city, at the lights in the distant smelters and mills, at the great hill opposite, with its slagdumps, gallows-frames and shaft-houses black against the dim light, which had yielded its millions and millions of tons of ore for the use of mankind. "All this had to be fought for. It didn't grow of itself. And because men fought for it, the place is what it is. Sixty thousand people live here, fed by the results of the battle. The highest wages in the world are paid the miners here. They live in rough comfort and plenty, whereas in the countries they came from they were underpaid and underfed. Is that not good?"

"Yes," she admitted.

"Life for you and for me must be different, thank God. You are in the world to makc for thc happiness of those you meet. That is good. But unless I am to run away from my work, what I do must make some unhappy. I can't help that if I am to do big things. When you hear people talking of the harm I do, you will remember what I have told you to-night, and you will think that a man and his work cannot be judged by isolated fragments."

"Yes," she breathed softly, for she knew that this man was saying good-by to her and was making his apologia.

"And you will remember that no matter how bitter the fight may grow between me and Mr. Harley, it has nothing to do with you. We shall still be friends, though we may never meet again."

"I shall remember that, too," he heard her murmur.

"You have been hoping that Mr. Harley and I would be friends. That is impossible. He came out here to crush me. For years his subordinates have tried to do this and failed. I am the only man alive that has ever resisted him successfully. I don't underestimate his power, which is greater than any czar or emperor that ever lived, but I don't think he will succeed. I shall win because I understand the forces against me. He will lose because he scorns those against him."

"I am sorry. Oh, I am so sorry," she wailed, gently as a breath of summer wind. For she saw now that the cleavage between them was too wide for a girl's efforts to bridge.

"That I am going to win?" he smiled gravely.

"That you must be enemies; that he came here to ruin you, since you say he did."

"You need not be too hard on him for that. By his code I am a freebooter and a highwayman. Business offers legitimate ways of robbery, and I transgress them. His ways are not my ways, and mine are not his, but it is only fair to say that his are the accepted ones."

"I don't understand it at all. You are both good men. I know you are. Surely you need not be enemies."

But she knew she could hope for no reassurance from the man beside her.

Presently she led him back across the big room to the fireplace near where her husband lay. His secretary had gone, and he was lying resting on the lounge. He opened his eyes and smiled at her. "Has Mr. Ridgway been pointing out to you the places of interest?" he asked quietly.

"Yes, dear." The last word came hesitantly after the slightest of pauses. "He says he must be going now."

The head of the greatest trust on earth got to his feet and smiled benignantly as he shook hands with the departing guest. "I shall hope to see you very soon and have a talk regarding business, Mr. Ridgway," he said.

"Whenever you like, Mr. Harley." To the girl he said merely, "Good night," and was gone.

The old man put an arm affectionately across his young wife's shoulder.

"Shall we read another psalm, my dear? Or are you tired?"

She repressed the little shiver that ran through her before she answered wearily. "I am a little tired. If you don't mind I would like to retire, please."

He saw her as far as the door of her apartments and left her with her maid after he had kissed the cold cheek she dutifully turned toward him.

CHAPTER 10

HARLEY MAKES A PROPOSITION

Apparently the head of the great trust intended to lose no time in having that business talk with Ridgway, which he had graciously promised the latter. Eaton and his chief were busy over some applications for leases when Smythe came into the room with a letter

"Messenger-boy brought it; said it was important," he explained.

Ridgway ripped open the envelope, read through the letter swiftly, and tossed it to Eaton. His eyes had grown hard and narrow

"Write to Mr. Hobart that I am sorry I haven't time to call on Mr. Harley at the Consolidated offices, as he suggests. Add that I expect to be in my offices all morning, and shall be glad to make an appointment to talk with Mr. Harley here, if he thinks he has any business with me that needs a personal interview."

Smythe's leathery face had as much expression as a blank wall, but Eaton gasped. The unparallcled audacity of flinging the billionaire's overture back in his face left him for the moment speechless. He knew that Ridgway had tempted Providence a hundred times without coming to disaster, but surely this was going too far. Any reasonable compromise with the great trust builder would be cause for felicitation. He had confidence in his chief to any point in reason, but he could not blind himself to the fact that the wonderful successes he had gained were provisional rather than final. He likened them to Stonewall Jackson's Shenandoah raid, very successful in irritating, disorganizing and startling the enemy, but with no serious bearing on the final inevitable result. In the end Harley would crush his foes if he set in motion the whole machinery of his limitless resources. That was Eaton's private opinion, and he was very much of the feeling that this was an opportune time to get in out of the rain.

"Don't you think we had better consider that answer before we send it, Waring?" he suggested in a low voice.

His chief nodded a dismissal to the secretary before answering.

"I have considered it."

"But—surely it isn't wise to reject his advances before we know what they are."

"I haven't rejected them. I've simply explained that we are doing business on equal terms. Even if I meant to compromise, it would pay me to let him know he doesn't own me."

"He may decide not to offer his proposition."

"It wouldn't worry me if he did."

Eaton knew he must speak now if his protest were to be of

any avail. "It would worry me a good deal. He has shown an inclination to be friendly. This answer is like a slap in the face."

"Is it?"

"Doesn't it look like that to you?"

Ridgway leaned back in his chair and looked thoughtfully at his friend. "Want to sell out, Steve?"

"Why—what do you mean?" asked the surprised treasurer.

"If you do, I'll pay anything in reason for your stock." He got up and began to pace the floor with long deliberate strides. "I'm a born gambler, Steve. It clears my head to take big chances. Give me a good fight on my hands with the chances against me, and I'm happy. You've got to take the world by the throat and shake success out of it if you're going to score heavily. That's how Harley made good years ago. Read the story of his life. See the chances he took. He throttled combinations a dozen times as strong as his. Some people say he was an accident. Don't you believe it. Accidents like him don't happen. He won because he was the biggest, brainiest, most daring and unscrupulous operator in the field. That's why I'm going to win—if I do win."

"Yes, if you win."

"Well, that's the chance I take," flung back the other as he swung buoyantly across the room. "But YOU don't need to take it. If you want, you can get out now at the top market price. I feel it in my bones I'm going to win; but if you don't feel it, you'd be a fool to take chances."

Eaton's mercurial temperament responded with a glow.

"No, sir. I'll sit tight. I'm no quitter."

"Good for you, Steve. I knew it. I'll tell you now that I would have hated like hell to see you leave me. You're the only man I can rely on down to the ground, twenty-four hours of every day."

The answer was sent, and Eaton's astonishment at his chief's temerity changed to amazement when the great Harley, pocketing his pride, asked for an appointment, and appeared at the offices of the Mesa Ore-producing Company at the time set. That Ridgway, who was busy with one of his superintendents, should actually keep the most powerful man in the country waiting in an outer office while he finished his business with Dalton seemed to him insolence florescent.

"Whom the gods would destroy," he murmured to himself as the only possible explanation, for the reaction of his enthusiasm was on him.

Nor did his chief's conference with Dalton show any leaning toward compromise. Ridgway had sent for his engineer to outline a program in regard to some ore-veins in the Sherman Bell, that had for months been in litigation between the two big interests at Mesa. Neither party to the suit had waited for the legal decision, but each of them had put a large force at work stoping out the ore. Occasional conflicts had occurred when the men of the opposing factions came in touch, as they frequently did, since crews were at work below and above each other at every level. But none of these as yet had been serious.

"Dalton, I was down last night to see that lease of Heyburn's on the twelfth level of the Taurus. The Consolidated will tap our workings about noon to-day, just below us. I want you to turn on them the air-drill pipe as soon as they break through.

Have a lot of loose rock there mixed with a barrel of lime. Let loose the air pressure full on the pile, and give it to their men straight. Follow them up to the end of their own tunnel when they retreat, and hold it against them. Get control of the levels above and below, too. Throw as many men as you can into their workings, and gut them till there is no ore left."

Dalton had the fighting edge. "You'll stand by me, no matter what happens?"

"Nothing will happen. They're not expecting trouble. But if anything does, I'll see you through. Eaton is your witness that I ordered it."

"Then it's as good as done, Mr. Ridgway," said Dalton, turning away.

"There may be bloodshed," suggested Eaton dubiously, in a low voice.

Ridgway's laugh had a touch of affectionate contempt. "Don't cross bridges till you get to them, Steve. Haven't you discovered, man, that the bold course is always the safe one? It's the quitter that loses out every time. The strong man gets there; the weak one falls down. It's as invariable as the law of gravity." He got up and stretched his broad shoulders in a deep breath. "Now for Mr. Harley. Send him in, Eaton.

That morning Simon Harley had done two things for many years foreign to his experience: He had gone to meet another man instead of making the man come to him, and he had waited the other man's pleasure in an outer office. That he had done so implied a strong motive.

Ridgway waved Harley to a chair without rising to meet him. The eyes of the two men fastened, wary and unwavering.

They might have been jungle beasts of prey crouching for the attack, so tense was their attention. The man from Broadway was the first to speak.

"I have called, Mr. Ridgway, to arrange, if possible, a compromise. I need hardly say this is not my usual method, but the circumstances are extremely unusual. I rest under so great a personal obligation to you that I am willing to overlook a certain amount of youthful presumption." His teeth glittered behind a lip smile, intended to give the right accent to the paternal reproof. "My personal obligation—"

"What obligation? I left you to die in the snow. "

"You forget what you did for Mrs. Harley."

"You may eliminate that," retorted the younger man curtly. "You are under no obligations whatever to me."

"That is very generous of you, Mr. Ridgway, but—"

Ridgway met his eyes directly, cutting his sentence as with a knife. "'Generous' is the last word to use. It is not a question of generosity at all. What I mean is that the thing I did was done with no reference whatever to you. It is between me and her alone. I refuse to consider it as a service to you, as having anything at all to do with you. I told you that before. I tell you again."

Harley's spirit winced. This bold claim to a bond with his wife that excluded him, the scornful thrust of his enemy—he was already beginning to consider him in that light rather than as a victim—had touched the one point of human weakness in this money-making Juggernaut. He saw himself for the moment without illusions, an old man and an unlovable one, without near kith or kin. He was bitterly aware that the child he had married had been sold to him by her guardian, under fear of imminent ruin, before her ignorance of the world had given her experience to judge for herself. The money and the hidden hunger of sentiment he wasted on her brought him only timid thanks and wan obedience. But for this man, with his hateful, confident youth, he had seen the warm smile touch her lips and the delicate color rose her cheeks. Nay, he had seen more her arms around his neck and her, warm breath on his cheek. They had lived romance, these two, in the days they had been alone together. They had shared danger and the joys of that Bohemia of youth from which he was forever excluded. It was his resolve to wipe out by financial favors—he could ruin the fellow later if need be—any claims of Ridgway upon her gratitude or her foolish imagination. He did not want the man's appeal upon her to carry the similitude of martyrdom as well as heroism.

"Yet, the fact remains that it was a service"—his thin lips smiled. "I must be the best judge of that, I think. I want to be perfectly frank, Mr. Ridgway. The Consolidated is an auxiliary enterprise so far as I am concerned, but I have always made it a rule to look after details when it became necessary. I came to Montana to crush you. I have always regarded you as a menace to our legitimate interests, and I had quite determined to make an end of it. You are a good fighter, and you've been on the ground in person, which counts for a great deal. But you must know that if I give myself to it in earnest, you are a ruined man."

The Westerner laughed hardily. "I hear you say it."

"But you don't believe," added the other quietly. "Many men have heard and not believed. They have KNOWN when it was too late.

"If you don't mind, I'll buy my experience instead of

borrowing it," Ridgway flung back flippantly.

"One moment, Mr. Ridgway. I have told you my purpose in coming to Montana. That purpose no longer exists. Circumstances have completely altered my intentions. The finger of God is in it. He has not brought us together thus strangely, except to serve some purpose of His own. I think I see that purpose. 'The stone which the builders refused is become the headstone of the corner. This is the Lord's doing; it is marvelous in our eyes,'" he quoted unctiously. "I am convinced that it is a waste of good material to crush you; therefore I desire to effect a consolidation with you, buy all the other copper interests of any importance in the country, and put you at the head of the resulting combination."

In spite of himself, Ridgway's face betrayed him. It was a magnificent opportunity, the thing he had dreamed of as the culmination of a lifetime of fighting. Nobody knew better than he on how precarious a footing he stood, on how slight a rock his fortunes might be wrecked. Here was his chance to enter that charmed, impregnable inner circle of finance that in effect ruled the nation. That Harley's suave friendliness would bear watching he did not doubt for a moment, but, once inside, so his vital youth told him proudly, he would see to it that the billionaire did not betray him. A week ago he could have asked nothing better than this chance to bloat himself into a some-day colossus. But now the thing stuck in his gorge. He understood the implied obligation. Payment for his service to Aline Harley was to be given, and the ledger balanced. Well, why not? Had he not spent the night in a chaotic agony of renunciation? But to renounce voluntarily was one thing, to be bought off another.

He looked up and met Harley's thin smile, the smile that on Wall Street was a synonym for rapacity and heartlessness, in the memory of which men had committed murder and suicide. On the instant there jumped between him and his ambition the face that had worked magic on him. What a God's pity that such a lamb should be cast to this ravenous wolf! He felt again her arms creeping round his neck, the divine trust of her lovely eyes. He had saved her when this man who called himself her husband had left her to perish in the storm. He had made her happy, as she had never been in all her starved life. Had she not promised never to forget, and was there not a deeper promise in her wistful eyes that the years could not wipe out? She was his by every right of natural law. By God! he would not sell his freedom of choice to this white haired robber!

"I seldom make mistakes in my judgment of men, Mr. Ridgway," the oily voice ran on. "No small share of such success as it has been given me to attain has been due to this instinct for putting my finger on the right man. I am assured that in you I find one competent for the great work lying before you. The opportunity is waiting; I furnish it, and you the untiring energy of youth to make the most of the chance." His wolfish smile bared the tusks for a moment. "I find myself not so young as I was. The great work I have started is well under way. I must trust its completion to younger and stronger hands than mine. I intend to rest, to devote myself to my home, more directly to such philanthropic and educational work as God has committed to my hands."

The Westerner gave him look for look, his eyes burning to get over the impasse of the expressionless mask no man had ever penetrated. He began to see why nobody had ever understood Harley. He knew there would be no rest for that consuming energy this side of the grave. Yet the man talked as if he believed his own glib lies.

"Consolidated is the watchword of the age; it means elimination of ruinous competition, and consequent harmony and reduced expense in management. Mr. Ridgway, may I count you with us? Together we should go far. Do you say peace or war?"

The younger man rose, leaning forward with his strong, sinewy hands gripping the table. His face was pale with the repression of a rage that had been growing intense. "I say war, and without quarter. I don't believe you can beat me. I defy you to the test. And if you should—even then I had rather go down fighting you than win at your side."

Simon Harley had counted acceptance a foregone conclusion, but he never winked a lash at the ringing challenge of his opponent. He met his defiance with an eye cold and steady as jade.

"As you please, Mr. Ridgway. I wash my hands of your ruin, and when you are nothing but a broken gambler, you will remember that I offered you the greatest chance that ever came to a man of your age. You are one of those men, I see, that would rather be first in hell than second in heaven. So be it." He rose and buttoned his overcoat.

"Say, rather, that I choose to go to hell my own master and not as the slave of Simon Harley," retorted the Westerner bitterly.

Ridgway's eyes blazed, but those of the New Yorker were cool and fishy.

"There is no occasion for dramatics," he said, the cruel, passionless smile at his thin lips. "I make you a business proposition and you decline it. That is all. I wish you good day."

The other strode past him and flung the door open. He had

never before known such a passion of hatred as raged within him. Throughout his life Simon Harley had left in his wake wreckage and despair. He was the best-hated man of his time, execrated by the working classes, despised by the country at large, and distrusted by his fellow exploiters. Yet, as a business opponent, Ridgway had always taken him impersonally, had counted him for a condition rather than an individual. But with the new influence that had come into his life, reason could not reckon, and when it was dominant with him, Harley stood embodied as the wolf ready to devour his ewe lamb.

For he couldn't get away from her. Wherever he went he carried with him the picture of her sweet, shy smile, her sudden winsome moments, the deep light in her violet eyes; and in the background the sinister bared fangs of the wild beast dogging her patiently, and yet lovingly.

CHAPTER 11

VIRGINIA INTERVENES

James K. Mott, local chief attorney for the Consolidated, was struggling with a white tie before the glass and crumpling it atrociously.

"This dress-suit habit is the most pernicious I know. It's sapping the liberties of the American people," he grunted at last in humorous despair.

"Let me, dear."

His wife tied it with neatness and dispatch, and returned to the inspection of how her skirt hung.

"Mr. Harley asked me to thank you for calling on his wife. He says she gets lonesome during the day while he is away so much. I was wondering if you couldn't do something for her so that she could meet some of the ladies of Mesa. A luncheon, or something of that sort, you know. Have you seen my hat-brush anywhere?"

"It's on that drawer beside your hat-box. She told me she would rather not. I suggested it. But I'll tell you what I could do: take Virginia Balfour round to see her. She's lively and good company, and knows some of the people Mrs. Harley knows."

"That's a good idea. I want Harley to know that we appreciate his suggestions, and are ready to do our part. He has shown a disposition to consult me on a good many things that ought to lie in Hobart's sphere rather than mine. Something's going to drop. Now, I like Hobart, but I want to show myself in a receptive mood for advancement when his head falls, as it certainly will soon."

* * * * * * *

Virginia responded eagerly to Mrs. Mott's suggestion that they call together on Mrs. Harley at the hotel.

"My dear, you have saved my life. I've been dying of curiosity, and I haven't been able to find vestige of an excuse to hang my call on. I couldn't ask Mr. Ridgway to introduce me, could I?"

"No, I don't see that you could," smiled Mrs. Mott, a motherly little woman with pleasant brown eyes. "I suppose Mr. Ridgway isn't exactly on calling terms with Mr. Harley's wife, even if he did save her life."

"Oh, Mr. Ridgway isn't the man to let a little thing like a war a outrance stand in the way of his social duties, especially when those duties happen to be inclinations, too. I understand he DID call the evening of their arrival here."

"He didn't!" screamed Mrs. Mott, who happened to possess a voice of the normal national register. "And what did Mr. Harley say?"

"Ah, that's what one would like to know. My informant

deponeth not beyond the fact unadorned. One may guess there must have been undercurrents of embarrassment almost as pronounced as if the President were to invite his Ananias Club to a pink tea. I can imagine Mr. Harley saying: 'Try this cake, Mr. Ridgway; it isn't poisoned;' and Mr. Ridgway answering: 'Thanks! After you, my dear Gaston.'"

Miss Balfour's anxiety to meet the young woman her fiance had rescued from the blizzard was not unnatural. Her curiosity was tinged with frank envy, though jealousy did not enter into it at all. Virginia had come West explicitly to take the country as she found it, and she had found it, unfortunately, no more hazardous than little old New York, though certainly a good deal more diverting to a young woman with democratic proclivities that still survived the energetic weeding her training had subjected them to.

She did not quite know what she had expected to find in Mesa. Certainly she knew that Indians were no longer on the map, and cowboys were kicking up their last dust before vanishing, but she had supposed that they had left compensations in their wake. On the principle that adventures are to the adventurous, her life should have been a whirl of hairbreadth escapes.

But what happened? She took all sorts of chances without anything coming of it. Her pirate fiance was the nearest approach to an adventure she had flushed, and this pink-and-white chit of a married schoolgirl had borrowed him for the most splendid bit of excitement that would happen in a hundred years. She had been spinning around the country in motor-cars for months without the sign of a blizzard, but the chit had hit one the first time. It wasn't fair. That was her blizzard by rights. In spirit, at least, she had "spoken for it," as she and her brother used to say when they were children of some coveted treasure not yet available. Virginia was

William MacLeod Raine

quite sure that if she had seen Waring Ridgway at the inspired moment when he was plowing through the drifts with Mrs. Harley in his arms—only, of course, it would have been she instead of Mrs. Harley, and he would not have been carrying her so long as she could stand and take it—she would have fallen in love with him on the spot. And those two days in the cabin on half-ration they would have put an end forever to her doubts and to that vision of Lyndon Hobart that persisted in her mind. What luck glace' some people did have!

But Virginia discovered the chit to be rather a different personality than she had supposed. In truth, she lost her heart to her at once. She could have stood out against Aline's mere good looks and been the stiffer for them. She was no MAN, to be moved by the dark hair's dusky glory, the charm of soft girlish lines, the effect of shy unsophistication that might be merely the highest art of social experience. But back of the sweet, trembling mouth that seemed to be asking to be kissed, of the pathetic appeal for friendliness from the big, deep violet eyes, was a quality of soul not to be counterfeited. Miss Balfour had furbished up the distant hauteur of the society manner she had at times used effectively, but she found herself instead taking the beautiful, forlorn little creature in her arms.

"Oh, my dear; my dear, how glad I am that dreadful blizzard did not hurt you!"

Aline clung to this gracious young queen as if she had known her a lifetime. "You are so good to me everybody is. You know how Mr. Ridgway saved me. If it had not been for him I should have died. I didn't care—I wanted to die in peace, I think—but he wouldn't let me."

"I should think not."

"If you only knew him—perhaps you do."

"A little," confessed Virginia, with a flash of merry eyes at Mrs. Mott.

"He is the bravest man—and the strongest."

"Yes. He is both," agreed his betrothed, with pride.

"His tenderness, his unselfishness, his consideration for others—did you ever know anybody like him for these things?"

"Never," agreed Virginia, with the mental reservations that usually accompanied her skeptical smile. She was getting at her fiance from a novel point of view.

"And so modest, with all his strength and courage.",

"It's almost a fault in him," she murmured.

"The woman that marries him will be blessed among women."

"I count it a great privilege," said Miss Balfour absently, but she pulled up with a hurried addendum: "To have known him."

"Indeed, yes. If one met more men like him this would be a better world."

"It would certainly be a different world."

It was a relief to Aline to talk, to put into words the external skeleton facts of the surging current that had engulfed her existence since she had turned a corner upon this unexpected consciousness of life running strong and deep. Harley was not a confidant she could have chosen under the most favorable circumstances, and her instinct told her that in this matter he was particularly impossible. But to Virginia Balfour—Mrs. Mott had to leave early to preside over the Mesa Woman's Club, and her friend allowed herself to be persuaded to stay longer—she did not find it at all hard to talk. Indeed, she murmured into the sympathetic ear of this astute young searcher of hearts more than her words alone said, with the result that Virginia guessed what she herself had not yet quite found out, though her heart was hovering tremblingly on the brink of discovery.

But Virginia's sympathy for the trouble fate had in store for this helpless innocent consisted with an alert appreciation of its obvious relation to herself. What she meant to discover was the attitude toward the situation of one neither particularly innocent nor helpless. Was he, too, about to be "caught in the coil of a God's romances," or was he merely playing on the vibrating strings of an untaught heart?

It was in part to satisfy this craving for knowledge that she wrote Ridgway a note as soon as she reached home. It said:

MY DEAR RECREANT LAGGARD: If you are not too busy playing Sir Lancelot to fair dames in distress, or splintering lances with the doughty husbands of these same ladies, I pray you deign to allow your servant to feast her eyes upon her lord's face. Hopefully and gratefully yours, VIRGINIA.

P. S.—Have you forgotten, sir, that I have not seen you since that terrible blizzard and your dreadful imprisonment in Fort Salvation?

P. P. S.—I have seen somebody else, though. She's a dear,

and full of your praises. I hardly blame you.

V.

She thought that ought to bring him soon, and it did.

"I've been busy night and day," he apologized when they met.

Virginia gave him a broadside demurely.

"I suppose your social duties do take up a good deal of your time."

"My social duties? Oh, I see!" He laughed appreciation of her hit. Evidently through her visit she knew a good deal more than he had expected. Since he had nothing to hide from her except his feelings, this did not displease him. "My duties in that line have been confined to one formal call."

She sympathized with him elaborately. "Calls of that sort do bore men so. I'll not forget the first time you called on me."

"Nor I," he came back gallantly.

"I marveled how you came through alive, but I learned then that a man can't be bored to death."

"I came again nevertheless," he smiled. "And again—and again."

"I am still wondering why."

"'Oh, wad some power the giffie gite us To see ourselves as others see us!'"

he quoted with a bow.

"Is that a compliment?" she asked dubiously.

"I have never heard it used so before. Anyhow, it is a little hackneyed for anybody so original as you."

"It was the best I could do offhand."

She changed the subject abruptly. "Has the new campaign of the war begun yet?"

"Well, we're maneuvering for position."

"You've seen him. How does he impress you?"

"The same as he does others. A hard, ruthless fighter. Unless all signs fail, he is an implacable foe."

"But you are not afraid?"

He smiled. "Do I look frightened?"

"No, you remind me of something a burglar once told me—"

"A what?"

"A burglar—a reformed burglar!" She gave him a saucy flash of her dark eyes. "Do you think I don't know any lawbreakers except those I have met in this State? I came across this one in a mission where I used to think I was doing good. He said it was not the remuneration of the profession that had attracted him, but the excitement. It was dreadfully frowned down upon and underpaid. He could earn more at his old trade of a locksmith, but it seemed to him that every impediment to success was a challenge to him. Poor man, he relapsed again, and they put him in Sing Sing. I was so interested in him, too."

"You've had some queer friends in your time," he laughed, but without a trace of disapproval.

"I have some queer ones yet," she thrust back.

"Let's not talk of them," he cried, in pretended alarm.

Her inextinguishable gaiety brought back the smile he liked. "We'll talk of SOME ONE else—some one of interest to us both."

"I am always ready to talk of Miss Virginia Balfour," he said, misunderstanding promptly.

She smiled her disdain of his obtuseness in an elaborately long survey of him.

"Well?" he wanted to know.

"That's how you look—very well, indeed. I believe the storm was greatly exaggerated," she remarked.

"Isn't that rather a good definition for a blizzard—a greatly exaggerated storm?"

"You don't look the worse for wear—not the wreck I expected to behold."

"Ah, you should have seen me before I saw you."

"Thank you. I have no doubt you find the sight of my dear face as refreshing as your favorite cocktail. I suppose that is why it has taken you three days after your return to reach me and then by special request."

"A pleasure delayed is twice a pleasure anticipation and realization."

Miss Balfour made a different application of his text, her eyes trained on him with apparent indifference. "I've been enjoying a delayed pleasure myself. I went to see her this afternoon."

He did not ask whom, but his eyes brightened.

"She's worth a good deal of seeing, don't you think?"

"Oh, I'm in love with her, but it doesn't follow you ought to be."

"Am I?"—he smiled.

"You are either in love or else you ought to be ashamed of yourself."

"An interesting thing about you is your point of view. Now, anybody else would tell me I ought to be ashamed if I am in love."

"I'm not worried about your morals," she scoffed. "It's that poor child I'm thinking of."

"I think of her a good deal, too."

"Ah! and does she think of you a good deal That's what we must guard against."

"Is it?"

"Yes. You see I'm her confidante." She told it him with sparkling eyes, for the piquancy of it amused her. Not every engaged young woman can hear her lover's praises sung by the woman whose life he has saved with the proper amount of romance.

"Really?"

She nodded, laughing at him. "I didn't get a chance to tell her about me."

"I suppose not."

"I think I'll tell her about you, though—just what a ruthless barbarian you are."

His eyes gleamed "I wish you would. I'd like to find out whether she would believe you. I have tried to tell her myself, but the honest truth is, I funk it."

"You haven't any right to let her know you are interested in her." She interrupted him before he could speak. "Don't trifle with her, Waring. She's not like other girls."

He met her look gravely. "I wouldn't trifle with her for any reason."

Her quick rejoinder overlapped his sentence. "Then you love her!"

"Is that an alternative?"

"With you—yes."

"Faith, my lady, you're frank!"

"I'm not mealy-mouthed. You don't think yourself scrupulous, do you?"

"I'm afraid I am not."

"I don't mind so much your being in love with HER, though it's not flattering to my vanity, but—" She stopped, letting him make the inference.

"Do you think that likely?" he asked, the color flushing his face.

He wondered how much Aline had told this confidante. Certain specific things he knew she had not revealed, but had she let her guess the situation between them?

She compromised with her conscience. "I don't know. She is romantic—and Simon Harley isn't a very fertile field for romance, I suppose."

"You would imply "

"Oh, you have points, and nobody knows them better than Waring Ridgway," she told him jauntily. "But you needn't play that role to the address of Aline Harley. Try ME. I'm immune to romance. Besides, I'm engaged to you," she added, laughing at the inconsequence the fact seemed to have for both of them.

"I'm afraid I can't help the situation, for if I've been playing a part, it has been an unconscious one."

"That's the worst of it. When you star as Waring Ridgway you are most dangerous. What I want is total abstinence."

"You'd rather I didn't see her at all?"

Virginia dimpled, a gleam of reminiscent laughter in her eyes. "When I was in Denver last month a Mrs. Smythe—it was Smith before her husband struck it rich last year—sent out cards for a bridge afternoon. A Mrs. Mahoney had just come to the metropolis from the wilds of Cripple Creek. Her husband had struck a gold-mine, too, and Mr. Smythe was under obligations to him. Anyhow, she was a stranger, and Mrs. Smythe took her in. It was Mrs. Mahoney's introduction to bridge, and she did not know she was playing for keeps. When the afternoon was over, Mrs. Smythe hovered about her with the sweetest sympathy. 'So sorry you had such a horrid run of cards, dear. Better luck next time.' It took Mrs. Mahoney some time to understand that her social afternoon had cost one hundred and twenty dollars, but next day her husband sent a check for one hundred and twenty-two dollars to Mrs. Smythe. The extra two dollars were for the refreshments, he naively explained, adding that since his wife was so poor a gambler as hardly to be able to keep professionals interested, he would not feel offended if Mrs. Smythe omitted her in future from her social functions."

Ridgway took it with a smile. "Simon Harley brought his one hundred and twenty-two dollars in person."

"He didn't! When?"

"This morning. He proposed benevolent assimilation as a solution of our troubles."

"Just how?"

"He offered to consolidate all the copper interests of the country and put me at the head of the resulting combine."

"If you wouldn't play bridge with Mrs. Harley?"

"Exactly."

"And you "

"Declined to pledge myself."

She clapped her hands softly. "Well done, Waring Ridgway! There are times when you are magnificent, when I could put you on a pedestal, you great big, unafraid man. But you mustn't play with her, just the same."

"Why mustn't I?"

"For her sake."

He frowned past her into space, his tight-shut jaw standing out saliently. "You're right, Virginia. I've been thinking so myself. I'll keep off the grass," he said, at last.

"You're a good fellow," slipped out impulsively.

"Well, I know where there's another," he said. "I ought to think myself a lucky dog."

Virginia lifted quizzical eyebrows. "Ought to! That tastes of duty. Don't let it come to that. We'll take it off if you like." She touched the solitaire he had given her.

"Ah, but I don't like"—he smiled.

CHAPTER 12

ALINE MAKES A DISCOVERY

Aline pulled her horse to a walk. "You know Mr. Ridgway pretty well, don't you?"

Miss Balfour gently flicked her divided skirt with a riding-whip, considering whether she might be said to know him well. "Yes, I think I do," she ventured.

"Mrs. Mott says you and he are great friends, that you seem very fond of each other."

"Goodness me! I hope I don't seem fond of him. I don't think 'fond' is exactly the word, anyway, though we are good friends." Quickly, keenly, her covert glance swept Aline; then, withdrawing her eyes, she flung her little bomb. "I suppose we may be said to appreciate each other. At any rate, we are engaged."

Mrs. Harley's pony came to an abrupt halt. "I thought I had dropped my whip," she explained, in a low voice not quite true.

Virginia, though she executed an elaborate survey of the scenery, could not help noticing that the color had washed from her friend's face. "I love this Western country—its big sweep of plains, of low, rolling hills, with a background of mountains. One can see how it gets into a man's blood so that the East seems insipid ever afterward," discoursed Miss Balfour.

A question trembled on Aline's blanched lips.

"Say it," permitted Virginia.

"Do you mean that you are engaged to him—that you are going to marry Mr. Ridgway—without caring for him?"

"I don't mean that at all. I like him immensely."

"But—do you love him?" It was almost a cry—these low words wrung from the tortured heart.

"No fair," warned her friend smilingly.

Aline rode in silence, her stricken face full of trouble. How could she, from her glass house, throw stones at a loveless marriage? But this was different from her own case! Nobody was worthy to marry her hero without giving the best a woman had to give. If she were a girl—a sudden tide of color swept her face; a wild, delirious tingle of joy flooded her veins—oh, if she were a girl, what a wealth of love could she give him! Clarity of vision had come to her in a blinding flash. Untutored of life, the knowledge of its meaning had struck home of the suddenest. She knew her heart now that it was too late; knew that she could never be indifferent to what concerned Waring Ridgway.

Aline caught at the courage behind her childishness, and accomplished her congratulations "You will be happy, I am sure. He is good."

"Goodness does not impress me as his most outstanding quality," smiled Miss Balfour.

"No, one never feels it emphasized. He is too He is too free of selfishness to make much of his goodness. But one can't help feeling it in everything he does and says."

"Does Mr. Harley agree with you? Does he feel it?"

"I don't think Mr. Harley understands him. I can't help thinking that he is prejudiced." She was becoming mistress of her voice and color again.

"And you are not?"

"Perhaps I am. In my thought of him he would still be good, even if he had done all the bad things his enemies accuse him of."

Virginia gave her up. This idealized interpretation of her betrothed was not the one she had, but for Aline it might be the true one. At least, she could not disparage him very consistently under the circumstances.

"Isn't there a philosophy current that we find in people what we look for in them? Perhaps that is why you and Mr. Harley read in Mr. Ridgway men so diverse as you do. It is not impossible you are both right and both wrong. Heaven knows, I suppose. At least, we poor mortals fog around enough when we sit in judgment." And Virginia shrugged the matter from her careless shoulders.

But Aline seemed to have a difficulty in getting away from the subject. "And you—what do you read?" she asked timidly.

"Sometimes one thing and sometimes another. To-day I see him as a living refutation of all the copy-book rules to success. He shatters the maxims with a touch-and-go manner that is fascinating in its immorality. A gambler, a plunger, an adventurer, he wins when a careful, honest business man would fail to a certainty."

Aline was amazed. "You misjudge him. I am sure you do. But if you think this of him why—"

"Why do I marry him? I have asked myself that a hundred times, my dear. I wish I knew. I have told you what I see in him to-day; but tomorrow—why, to-morrow I shall see him an altogether different man. He will be perhaps a radiating center of altruism, devoted to his friends, a level-headed protector of the working classes, a patron of the arts in his own clearminded, unlettered way. But whatever point of view one gets at him, he spares one dullness. Will you explain to me, my dear, why picturesque rascality is so much more likable than humdrum virtue?"

Mrs. Harley's eyes blazed. "And you can talk this way of the man you are going to marry, a man—" She broke off, her voice choked.

Miss Balfour was cool as a custard. "I can, my dear, and without the least disloyalty. In point of fact, he asked me to tell you the kind of man I think him. I'm trying to oblige him, you see."

"He asked you—to tell me this about him?" Aline pulled in her pony in order to read with her astonished eyes the amused ones of her companion.

"Yes. He was afraid you were making too much of his saving you. He thinks he won't do to set on a pedestal."

"Then I think all the more of him for his modesty."

"Don't invest too heavily on his modesty, my dear. He wouldn't be the man he is if he owned much of that commodity."

"The man he is?"

"Yes, the man born to win, the man certain of himself no matter what the odds against him.

He knows he is a man of destiny; knows quite well that there is something big about him that dwarfs other men. I know it, too. Wherefore I seize my opportunity. It would be a sin to let a man like that get away from one. I could never forgive myself," she concluded airily.

"Don't you see any human, lovable things in him?" Aline's voice was an accusation.

"He is the staunchest friend conceivable. No trouble is too great for him to take for one he likes, and where once he gives his trust he does not take it back. Oh, for all his force, he is intensely human! Take his vanity, my dear. It soars to heaven."

"If I cared for him I couldn't dissect his qualities as you do."

"That's because you are a triumph of the survival of nature and impulse over civilization, in spite of its attempts to sap your freshness. For me, I fear I'm a sophisticated daughter of a critical generation. If I weren't, I should not hold my judgment so safely in my own keeping, but would surrender it and my heart."

"There is something about the way you look at him that shocks me. One ought not to let oneself believe all that seems easy to believe."

"That is your faith, but mine is a different one. You see, I'm a Unitarian," returned Virginia blithely.

"He will make you love him if you marry him," sighed Aline, coming back to her obsession.

Virginia nodded eagerly. "In my secret heart that is what I am hoping for, my dear."

"Unless there is another man," added Aline, as if alone with her thoughts.

Virginia was irritably aware of a flood of color beating into her cheeks. "There isn't any other man," she said impatiently.

Yet she thought of Lyndon Hobart. Curiously enough, whenever she conceived herself as marrying Ridgway, the reflex of her brain carried to her a picture of Hobart, clean-handed, fine of instinct, with the inherited inflections of voice and unconscious pride of caste that come from breeding and not from cultivation. If he were not born to greatness, like his rival, at least he satisfied her critical judgment of what a gentleman should be; and she was quite sure that the potential capacity lay in her to care a good deal more for him than for anybody else she had met. Since it was not on the cards, as Miss Virginia had shuffled the pack, that she should marry primarily for reasons sentimental, this annoyed her in her sophisticated hours.

But in the hours when she was a mere girl when she was not so confidently the heir of all the feminine wisdom of the ages, her annoyance took another form. She had told Lyndon Hobart of her engagement because it was the honest thing to do; because she supposed she ought to discourage any hopes he might be entertaining. But it did not follow that he need have let these hopes be extinguished so summarily. She could have wished his scrupulous regard for the proper thing had not had the effect of taking him so completely out of her external life, while leaving him more insistently than ever the subject of her inner contemplation.

Virginia's conscience was of the twentieth century and American, though she was a good deal more honest with herself than most of her sex in the same social circle. Also she was straightforward with her neighbors so far as she could reasonably be. But she was not a Puritan in the least, though she held herself to a more rigid account than she did her friends. She judged her betrothed as little as she could, but this was not to be entirely avoided, since she expected her life to become merged so largely in his. There were hours when she felt she must escape the blighting influence of his lawlessness. There were others when it seemed to her magnificent.

Except for the occasional jangle of a bit or the ring of a horse's shoe on a stone, there was silence which lasted many minutes. Each was busy with her thoughts, and the narrowness of the trail, which here made them go in single file, served as an excuse against talk.

"Perhaps we had better turn back," suggested Virginia, after the path had descended to a gulch and merged itself in a wagon-road. "We shall have no more than time to get home and dress for dinner."

Aline turned her pony townward, and they rode at a walk side by side.

"Do you know much about the difficulty between Mr. Harley and Mr. Ridgway? I mean about the mines—the Sherman

Bell, I think they called it?"

"I know something about the trouble in a general way. Both the Consolidated and Mr. Ridgway's company claim certain veins. That is true of several mines, I have been told."

"I don't know anything about business. Mr. Harley does not tell me anything about his. To day I was sitting in the open window, and two men stopped beneath it. They thought there would be trouble in this mine—that men would be hurt. I could not make it all out, but that was part of it. I sent for Mr. Harley and made him tell me what he knew. It would be dreadful if anything like that happened."

"Don't worry your head about it, my dear. Things are always threatening and never happening. It seems to be a part of the game of business to bluff, as they call it."

"I wish it weren't," sighed the girl-wife.

Virginia observed that she looked both sad and weary. She had started on her ride like a prisoner released from his dungeon, happy in the sunshine, the swift motion, the sting of the wind in her face. There had been a sparkle in her eye and a ring of gaiety in her laugh. Into her cheeks a faint color had glowed, so that the contrast of their clear pallor with the vivid scarlet of the little lips had been less pronounced than usual. But now she was listless and distraite, the girlish abandon all stricken out of her. It needed no clairvoyant to see that her heart was heavy and that she was longing for the moment when she could be alone with her pain.

Her friend had learned what she wanted to know, and the knowledge of it troubled her. She would have given a good deal to have been able to lift this sorrow from the girl riding beside her. For she was aware that Aline Harley might as well have reached for the moon as that toward which her untutored heart yearned. She had come to life late and traveled in it but a little way. Yet the tragedy of it was about to engulf her. No lifeboat was in sight. She must sink or swim alone. Virginia's unspoiled heart went out to her with a rush of pity and sympathy. Almost the very words that Waring Ridgway had used came to her lips.

"You poor lamb! You poor, forsaken lamb!"

But she spoke instead with laughter and lightness, seeing nothing of the girl's distress, at least, until after they separated at the door of the hotel.

CHAPTER 13

FIRST BLOOD

After Ridgway's cavalier refusal to negotiate a peace treaty, Simon Harley and his body-guard walked back to the offices of the Consolidated, where they arrived at the same time as the news of the enemy's first blow since the declaration of renewed war.

Hobart was at his desk with his ear to the telephone receiver when the great financier came into the inner office of the manager.

"Yes. When? Driven out, you say? Yes—yes. Anybody hurt? Followed our men through into our tunnel? No, don't do anything till you hear from me. Send Rhys up at once. Let me know any further developments that occur."

Hobart hung up the receiver and turned on his swivel-chair toward his chief. "Another outrage, sir, at the hands of Ridgway. It is in regard to those veins in the Copper King that he claims. Dalton, his superintendent of the Taurus, drove a tunnel across our lateral lines and began working them, though their own judge has not yet rendered a decision in their favor.

Of course, I put a large force in them at once. To-day we tapped their workings at the twelfth level. Our foreman, Miles, has just telephoned me that Dalton turned the air pressure on our men, blew out their candles, and flung a mixture of lime and rocks at them. Several of the men are hurt, though none badly. It seems that Dalton has thrown a force into our tunnels and is holding the entrances against us at the point where the eleventh, twelfth, and thirteenth levels touch the cage. It means that he will work those veins, and probably others that are acknowledged to be ours, unless we drive them out, which would probably be a difficult matter."

Harley listened patiently, eyes glittering and clean-shaven lips pressed tightly against his teeth. "What do you propose to do?"

"I haven't decided yet. If we could get any justice from the courts, an injunction "

"Can't be got from Purcell. Don't waste time considering it. Fight it out yourself. Find his weakest spot, then strike hard and suddenly." Harley's low metallic voice was crisp and commanding.

"His weakest spot?"

"Exactly. Has he no mines upon which we can retaliate?"

"There is the Taurus. It lies against the Copper King end to end. He drove a tunnel into some of our workings last winter. That would give a passageway to send our men through, if we decide to do so. Then there is his New York. Its workings connect with those of the Jim Hill."

"Good! Send as many men through as is necessary to capture and hold both mines. Get control of the entire workings of them both, and begin taking ore out at once. Station armed guards at every point where it is necessary, and as many as are necessary. Use ten thousand men, if you need that many. But don't fail. We'll give Ridgway a dose of his own medicine, and teach him that for every pound of our ore he steals we'll take ten."

"He'll get an injunction from the courts."

"Let him get forty. I'll show him that his robber courts will not save him. Anyhow, we'll cross that bridge when we come to it."

Hobart, almost swept from his moorings by the fiery energy of his chief, braced himself to withstand the current.

"I shall have to think about that. We can't fight lawlessness with lawlessness except for selfpreservation."

"Think! You do nothing but think, Mr. Hobart. You are here to act," came the scornful retort; "And what is this but self-preservation."

"I am willing to recapture our workings in the Copper King. I'll lead the attack in person, sir. But as to a retaliatory attack—the facts will not justify a capture of his property because he has seized ours."

"Wrong, sir. This is no time for half-way measures. I have resolved to crush this freebooter; since he has purchased your venal courts, then by the only means left us—force."

Hobart rose from his seat, very pale and erect. His eyes met those of the great man unflinchingly. "You realize that this may mean murder, Mr. Harley? That a clash cannot possibly be avoided if you pursue this course?"

"I realize that it is self-preservation," came the cold retort. "There is no law here, none, at least, that gives us justice. We are back to savagery, dragged back by the madness of this ruffian. It is his choice, not mine. Let him abide by it."

"Your intention to follow this course is irrevocable?"

"Absolutely."

"In that case, I must regretfully offer my resignation as manager of the Consolidated."

"It is accepted, Mr. Hobart. I can't have men working under me that are not loyal, body and soul, to the hand that feeds them. No man can serve two masters, Mr. Hobart."

"That is why I resign, Mr. Harley. You give me the devil's work to do. I have done enough of it. By Heaven, I will be a free man hereafter." The disgust and dissatisfaction that had been pent within him for many a month broke forth hot from the lips of this self-repressed man. "It is all wrong on both sides. Two wrongs do not make a right. The system of espionage we employ over everybody both on his side and ours, the tyrannical use we make of our power, the corruption we foster in politics, our secret bargains with railroads, our evasions of law as to taxes, and in every other way that suits us: it is all wrong—all wrong. I'll be a party to it no longer. You see to what it leads—murder and anarchy. I'll be a poor man if I must, but I'll be a free and honest one at least."

"You are talking wickedly and wildly, Mr. Hobart. You are criticizing God when you criticize the business conditions he has put into the world. I did not know that you were a socialist, but what you have just said explains your course," the old man reproved sadly and sanctimonious.

"I am not a socialist, Mr. Harley, but you and your methods have made thousands upon thousands of them in this country during the past ten years."

"We shall not discuss that, Mr. Hobart, nor, indeed, is any discussion necessary. Frankly, I am greatly disappointed in you. I have for some time been dissatisfied with your management, but I did not, of course, know you held these anarchistic views. I want, however, to be perfectly just. You are a very good business man indeed, careful and thorough. That you have not a bold enough grasp of mind for the place you hold is due, perhaps, to these dangerous ideas that have unsettled you. Your salary will be continued for six months. Is that satisfactory?"

"No, sir. I could not be willing to accept it longer than to-day. And when you say bold enough, why not be plain and say unscrupulous enough?" amended the younger man.

"As you like. I don't juggle with words. The point is, you don't succeed. This adventurer, Ridgway, scores continually against you. He has beaten you clear down the line from start to finish. Is that not true?"

"Because he does not hesitate to stoop to anything, because—"

"Precisely. You have given the very reason why he must be fought in the same spirit. Business ethics would be as futile against him as chivalry in dealing with a jungle-tiger."

"You would then have had me stoop to any petty meanness to win, no matter how contemptible?"

The New Yorker waved him aside with a patient, benignant gesture. "I don't care for excuses. I ask of my subordinates success. You do not get it for me. I must find a man who can."

Hobart bowed with fine dignity. The touch of disdain in his slight smile marked his sense of the difference between them. He was again his composed rigid self.

"Can you arrange to allow my resignation to take effect as soon as possible? I should prefer to have my connection with the company severed before any action is taken against these mines."

"At once—to-day. Your resignation may be published in the Herald this afternoon, and you will then be acquitted of whatever may follow."

"Thank you." Hobart hesitated an instant before he said: "There is a point that I have already mentioned to you which, with your permission, I must again advert to. The temper of the miners has been very bitter since you refused to agree to Mr. Ridgway's proposal for an eight-hour day. I would urge upon you to take greater precautions against a personal attack. You have many lawless men among your employees. They are foreigners for the most part, unused to self-restraint. It is only right you should know they execrate your name."

The great man smiled blandly. "Popularity is nothing to me. I have neither sought it nor desired it. Given a great work to do, with the Divine help I have done it, irrespective of public clamor. For many years I have lived in the midst of alarms, Mr. Hobart. I am not foolhardy. What precautions I can reasonably take I do. For the rest, my confidence is in an all-wise Providence. It is written that not even a sparrow falls without His decree. In that promise I put my trust. If I am to be cut off it can only be by His will. 'The Lord gave, and the

Lord hath taken away; blessed be the name of the Lord.' Such, I pray, may be the humble and grateful spirit with which I submit myself to His will."

The retiring manager urged the point no further. "If you have decided upon my successor and he is on the ground I shall be glad to give the afternoon to running over with him the affairs of the office. It would be well for him to retain for a time my private secretary and stenographer."

"Mr. Mott will succeed you. He will no doubt be glad to have your assistance in helping him fall into the routine of the office, Mr. Hobart."

Harley sent for Mott at once and told him of his promotion. The two men were closeted together for hours, while trusted messengers went and came incessantly to and from the mines. Hobart knew, of course, that plans were in progress to arm such of the Consolidated men as could be trusted, and that arrangements were being made to rush the Taurus and the New York. Everything was being done as secretly as possible, but Hobart's experience of Ridgway made it obvious to him that this excessive activity could not pass without notice. His spies, like those of the trust, swarmed everywhere.

It was not till mid-afternoon of the next day that Mott found time to join him and run over with him the details of such unfinished business as the office had taken up. The retiring manager was courtesy itself, nor did he feel any bitterness against his successor. Nevertheless, he came to the end of office hours with great relief. The day had been a very hard one, and it left him with a longing for solitude and the wide silent spaces of the open hills. He struck out in the direction which promised him the quickest opportunity to leave the town behind him. A good walker, he covered the miles rapidly, and under the physical satisfaction of the tramp the brain knots unraveled and smoothed themselves out. It was better so—better to live his own life than the one into which he was being ground by the inexorable facts of his environment. He was a young man and ambitious, but his hopes were not selfish. At bottom he was an idealist, though a practical one. He had had to shut his eyes to many things which he deplored, had been driven to compromises which he despised. Essentially clean-handed, the soul of him had begun to wither at the contact of that which he saw about him and was so large a part of.

"I am not fit for it. That is the truth. Mott has no imagination, and property rights are the most sacred thing on earth to him. He will do better at it than I," he told himself, as he walked forward bareheaded into the great sunset glow that filled the saddle between two purple hills in front of him.

As he swung round a bend in the road a voice, clear and sweet. came to him through the light filtered air.

"Laska!"

young woman on horseback was before him. Her pony stood across the road, and she looked up a trail which ran down into it. The lifted poise of the head brought out its fine lines and the distinction with which it was set upon the well-molded throat column. Apparently she was calling to some companion on the trail who had not yet emerged into view.

At sound of his footsteps the rider's head turned.

"Good afternoon, Mr. Hobart," she said quietly, as coolly as if her heart had not suddenly begun to beat strangely fast.

"Good afternoon, Miss Balfour."

Each of them was acutely conscious of the barrier between them. Since the day when she had told him of her engagement they had not met, even casually, and this their first sight of each other was not without embarrassment.

"We have been to Lone Pine Cone," she said rather hurriedly, to bridge an impending silence.

He met this obvious statement with another as brilliant.

"I walked out from town. My horse is a little lame."

But there was something she wanted to say to him, and the time for saying it, before the arrival of her companion, was short. She would not waste it in commonplaces.

"I don't usually read the papers very closely, but this morning I read both the Herald and the Sun. Did you get my note?"

"Your note? No."

"I sent it by mail. I wanted you to know that your friends are proud of you. We know why you resigned. It is easy to read between the lines."

"Thank you," he said simply. "I knew you would know."

"Even the Sun recognizes that it was because you are too good a man for the place."

"Praise from the Sun has rarely shone my way," he said, with a touch of irony, for that paper was controlled by the Ridgway interest. "In its approval I am happy."

Her impulsive sympathy for this man whom she so greatly

liked would not accept the rebuff imposed by this reticence. She stripped the gauntlet from her hand and offered it in congratulation.

He took it in his, a slight flush in his face.

"I have done nothing worthy of praise. One cannot ask less of a man than that he remain independent and honest. I couldn't do that and stay with the Consolidated, or, so it seemed to me. So I resigned. That is all there is to it."

"It is enough. I don't know another man would have done it, would have had the courage to do it after his feet were set so securely in the way of success. The trouble with Americans is that they want too much success. They want it at too big a price."

"I'm not likely ever to have too much of it," he laughed sardonically.

"Success in life and success in living aren't the same thing. It is because you have discovered this that you have sacrificed the less for the greater." She smiled, and added: "I didn't mean that to sound as preachy as it does."

"I'm afraid you make too much of a small thing. My squeamishness has probably made me the laughing-stock of Mesa."

"If so, that is to the discredit of Mesa," she insisted stanchly. "But I don't think so. A great many people who couldn't have done it themselves will think more of you for having done it."

Another pony, which had been slithering down the steep trail in the midst of a small rock slide, now brought its rider safely to a halt in the road. Virginia introduced them, and

Hobart, remembered that he had heard Miss Balfour speak of a young woman whom she had met on the way out, a Miss Laska Lowe, who was coming to Mesa to teach domestic science in the public schools. There was something about the young teacher's looks that he liked, though she was of a very different type than Virginia. Not at all pretty in any accepted sense, she yet had a charm born of the vital honesty in her. She looked directly at one out of sincere gray eyes, wide-awake and fearless. As it happened, her friend had been telling her about Hobart, and she was interested in him from the first. For she was of that minority which lives not by bread alone, and she felt a glow of pride in the man who could do what the Sun had given this man credit for editorially.

They talked at haphazard for a few minutes before the young women cantered away. As Hobart trudged homeward he knew that in the eyes of these two women, at least, he had not been a fool.

CHAPTER 14

A CONSPIRACY

Tucked away in an obscure corner of the same issue of the papers which announced the resignation of Lyndon Hobart as manager of the Consolidated properties, and the appointment of James K. Mott as his temporary successor, were little one-stick paragraphs regarding explosions, which had occurred the night before in tunnels of the Taurus and the New York. The general public paid little attention to these, but those on the inside knew that Ridgway had scored again. His spies had carried the news to him of the projected capture of these two properties by the enemy. Instead of attempting to defend them by force, he had set of charges of giant powder which had brought down the tunnel roofs and effectually blocked the entrances from the Consolidated mines adjoining.

With the indefatigable patience which characterized him, Harley set about having the passages cleared of the rock and timber with which they were filled. Before he had succeeded in doing this his enemy struck another telling blow. From Judge Purcell he secured an injunction against the Consolidated from working its mines, the Diamond King, the Mary K, and the Marcus Daly, on the absurd contention that the principal ore-vein of the Marcus Daly apexed on the tin, triangle wedged in between these three great mines, and called by Ridgway the Trust Buster. Though there was not room enough upon this fragment to sink a shaft, it was large enough to found this claim of a vein widening as it descended until it crossed into the territory of each of these properties. Though Harley could ignore court injunctions which erected only under-ground territory, he was forced to respect this one, since it could not be violated except in the eyes of the whole country. The three mines closed down, and several thousand workmen were thrown out of employment. These were immediately reemployed by Ridgway and set to work both in his own and the Consolidated's territory.

Within a week a dozen new suits were instituted against the Consolidated by its enemy. He harassed it by contempt proceedings, by applications for receiverships, and by other ingenious devices, which greatly tormented the New York operator. For the first time in his life the courts, which Harley had used to much advantage in his battles to maintain and extend the trusts he controlled, could not be used even to get scant justice.

Meanwhile both leaders were turning their attention to the political situation. The legislators were beginning to gather for the coming session, and already the city was full of rumors about corruption. For both the Consolidated and its enemy were making every effort to secure enough votes to win the election of a friendly United States senator. The man chosen would have the distribution of the federal patronage of the State. This meant the control of the most influential local politicians of the party in power at Washington as well as their followers, an almost vital factor for success in a State where political corruption had so interwoven itself into the business life of the community.

The hotel lobbies were filled with politicians gathered from every county in the State. Big bronzed cattlemen brushed shoulders with budding lawyers from country towns and ward bosses from the larger cities. The bars were working overtime, and the steady movement of figures in the corridors lasted all day and most of the night. Here and there were collected groups, laughing and talking about the old frontier days, or commenting in lowered tones on some phase of the feverish excitement that was already beginning to be apparent. Elevators shot up and down, subtracting and adding to the kaleidoscope of human life in the rotundas. Bellboys hurried to and fro with messages and cocktails. The ring of the telephone-bell cut occasionally into the deep hum of many voices. All was confusion, keen interest, expectancy.

For it was known that Simon Harley had sent for $300,000 in cold cash to secure the election of his candidate, Roger D. Warner, a lawyer who had all his life been close to corporate interests. It was known, too, that Waring Ridgway had gathered together every element in the State that opposed the domination of the Consolidated, to fight their man to a finish. Bets for large sums were offered and taken as to the result, heavy odds being given in favor of the big copper trust's candidate. For throughout the State at large the Consolidated influence was very great indeed. It owned forest lands and railroads and mines. It controlled local transportation largely. Nearly one-half the working men in the State were in its employ. Into every town and village the ramifications of its political organization extended. The feeling against it was very bitter, but this was usually expressed in whispers. For it was in a position to ruin almost any business man upon whom it fastened a grudge, and to make wealthy any upon whom it chose to cast its favors.

Nevertheless, there were some not so sure that the Consolidated would succeed in electing its man. Since Ridgway had announced himself as a candidate there had been signs of defection on the part of some of those expected to vote for Warner. He had skillfully wielded together in opposition to the trust all the elements of the State that were hostile to it; and already the word was being passed that he had not come to the campaign without a barrel of his own.

The balloting for United States senator was not to begin until the eighth day of the session, but the opening week was full of a tense and suppressed excitement. It was known that agents of both sides were moving to and fro among the representatives and State senators, offering fabulous prices for their votes and the votes of any others they might be able to control. Men who had come to the capital confident in their strength and integrity now looked at their neighbors furtively and guiltily. Day by day the legislators were being debauched to serve the interest of the factions which were fighting for control of the State. Night after night secret meetings were being held in out-of-the-way places to seduce those who clung desperately to their honesty or held out for a bigger price. Bribery was in the air, rampant, unashamed. Thousand-dollar bills were as common as ten-dollar notes in ordinary times.

Sam Yesler, commenting on the situation to his friend Jack Roper, a fellow member of the legislature who had been a cattleman from the time he had given up driving a stage thirty years before, shook his head dejectedly over his blue points.

"I tell you, Jack, a man has to be bed-rocked in honesty or he's gone. Think of it. A country lawyer comes here who has never seen five thousand dollars in a lump sum, and they shove fifteen thousand at him for his vote. He is poor, ambitious, struggling along from hand to mouth. I reckon we ain't in a position to judge that poor devil of a harassed fellow. Mebbe he's always been on the square, came here to do what was right, we'll say, but he sees corruption all round him. How can he help getting a warped notion of things? He sees his friends and his neighbors falling by the wayside. By God, it's got to the point in this legislature that an honest man's an object of obloquy."

"That's right," agreed Roper. "Easy enough for us to be square. We got good ranches back of us and can spend the winter playing poker at the Mesa Club if we feel like it. But if we stood where Billy George and Garner and Roberts and Munz do, I ain't so damn sure my virtue would stand the strain. Can you reach that salt, Sam?"

"Billy George has got a sick wife, and he's been wanting to send her back to her folks in the East, but he couldn't afford it. The doctors figured she ought to stay a year, and Billy would have to hire a woman to take care of his kids. I said to him: 'Hell, Billy, what's a friend for?' And I shoves a check at him. He wouldn't look at it; said he didn't know whether he could ever pay it, and he had not come down to charity yet."

"Billy's a white man. That's what makes me sick. Right on top of all his bad luck he comes here and sees that everybody is getting a big roll. He thinks of that white-faced wife of his dragging herself round among the kids and dying by inches for lack of what money can buy her. I tell you I don't blame him. It's the fellows putting the temptation up to him that ought to be strung up."

"I see that hound Pelton's mighty active in it. He's got it in for Ridgway since Waring threw him down, and he's plugging night and day for Warner. Stays pretty well tanked up. Hopper tells me he's been making threats to kill Waring on sight."

"I heard that and told Waring. He laughed and said he hoped he would live till Pelton killed him. I like Waring. He's got the guts, as his miners say. But he's away off on this fight. He's using money right and left just as Harley is."

Yesler nodded. "The whole town's corrupted. It takes bribery for granted. Men meet on the street and ask what the price of votes is this morning. Everybody feels prosperous."

"I heard that a chambermaid at the Quartzite Hotel found seven thousand dollars in big bills pinned to the bottom of a mattress in Garner's room yesterday. He didn't dare bank it, of course."

"Poor devil! He's another man that would like to be honest, but with the whole place impregnated with bribery he couldn't stand the pressure. But after this is all over he'll go home to his wife and his neighbors with the canker of this thing at his heart until he dies. I tell you, Jack, I'm for stopping it if we can."

"How?"

"There's one way. I've been approached indirectly by Pelton, to deliver our vote to the Consolidated. Suppose we arrange to do it, get evidence, and make a public exposure."

They were alone in a private dining-room of a restaurant, but Yesler's voice had fallen almost to a whisper. With his steady gray eyes he looked across at the man who had ridden the range with him fifteen years ago when he had not had a sou to bless himself with.

Roper tugged at his long drooping mustache and gazed at his friend. "It's a large order, Sam, a devilish large order. Do you reckon we could deliver?"

"I think so. There are six of us that will stand pat at any cost. If we play our cards right and keep mum the surprise of it is bound to shake votes loose when we spring the bomb. The whole point is whether we can take advantage of that surprise to elect a decent man. I don't say it can be done, but there's a chance of it."

The old stage-driver laughed softly. "We'll be damned good and plenty by both sides."

"Of course. It won't be a pleasant thing to do, but then it isn't exactly pleasant to sit quiet and let these factions use the State as a pawn in their game of grab."

"I'm with you, Sam. Go to it, my boy, and I'll back you to the limit."

"We had better not talk it over here. Come to my room after dinner and bring Landor and James with you. I'll have Reedy and Keller there. I'll mention casually that it's a big game of poker, and I'll have cards and drinks sent up. You want to remember we can't be too careful. If it leaks out we lose."

"I'm a clam, Sam. Do you want I should speak of it to Landor and James?"

"Better wait till we get together."

"What about Ward? He's always been with us."

"He talks too much. We can take him in at the last minute if we like."

"That would be better. I ain't so sure about Reedy, either. He's straight as a string, of course; not a crooked hair in his head. But when he gets to drinking he's likely to let things out."

"You're right. We'll leave him out, too, until the last minute. There's another thing I've thought of. Ridgway can't win. At least I don't see how he can control more than twenty five votes. Suppose at the very last moment we make a deal with him and with the Democrats to pool our votes on some square man. With Waring it's anything to beat the Consolidated. He'll jump at the chance if he's sure he is out of the running himself. Those of the Democrats that Harley can't buy will be glad to beat his man. I don't say it can be done, Jack. All I say is that it is worth a trial."

"You bet."

They met that night in Yesler's rooms round a card-table. The hands were dealt for form's sake, since there were spies everywhere, and it was necessary to ring for cigars and refreshments occasionally to avoid suspicion. They were all cattlemen, large or small, big outdoors sunburned men, who rode the range in the spring and fall with their punchers and asked no odds of any man.

Until long past midnight they talked the details over, and when they separated in the small hours it was with a well-defined plan to save the State from its impending disgrace if the thing could be done.

CHAPTER 15

LASKA OPENS A DOOR

The first ballots for a United States senator taken by the legislature in joint session failed to disclose the alignment of some of the doubtful members. The Democratic minority of twenty-eight votes were cast for Springer, the senator whose place would be taken by whoever should win in the contest now on. Warner received forty-four, Ridgway twenty-six, eight went to Pascom, a former governor whom the cattle-men were supporting, and the remaining three were scattered. Each day one ballot was taken, and for a week there was a slight sifting down of the complimentary votes until at the end of it the count stood:

Warner	45
Ridgway	28
Springer	28
Pascom	8

Warner still lacked ten votes of an election, but It was pretty thoroughly understood that several of the Democratic minority were waiting only long enough for a colorable excuse to switch to him. All kinds of rumors were in the air as to how many of these there were. The Consolidated leaders boldly claimed that they had only to give the word to force the election of their candidate on any ballot. Yesler did not believe this claim could be justified, since Pelton and Harley were already negotiating with him for the delivery of the votes belonging to the cattlemen's contingent.

He had held off for some time with hints that it would take a lot of money to swing the votes of such men as Roper and Landor, but he had finally come to an agreement that the eight votes should be given to Warner for a consideration of $300,000. This was to be paid to Yesler in the presence of the other seven members on the night before the election, and was to be held in escrow by him and Roper until the pact was fulfilled, the money to be kept in a safety deposit vault with a key in possession of each of the two.

On the third day of the session, before the voting had begun, Stephen Eaton, who was a State senator from Mesa, moved that a committee be appointed to investigate the rumors of bribery that were so common. The motion caught the Consolidated leaders napping, for this was the last man they had expected to propose such a course, and it went through with little opposition, as a similar motion did in the House at the same time. The lieutenant-governor and the speaker of the House were both opposed to Warner, and the joint committee had on it the names of no Consolidated men. The idea of such a committee had originated with Ridgway, and had been merely a bluff to show that he at least was willing that the world should know the whole story of the election. Nor had this committee held even formal meetings before word reached Eaton through Yesler that if it would appoint a conference in some very private place, evidence would be submitted implicating agents of the Warner forces in attempts at bribery.

It was close to eleven o'clock when Sam Yesler stepped quietly from a side door of his hotel and slipped into the street. He understood perfectly that in following the course he did, he was taking his life in his hands. The exposure of the bribery traffic would blast forever the reputations of many men who had hitherto held a high place in the community, and he knew the temper of some of them well enough to be aware that an explosion was probable. Spies had been dogging him ever since the legislature convened. Within an hour one of them would be flying to Pelton with the news that he was at a meeting of the committee, and all the thugs of the other side would be turned loose on his heels. As he walked briskly through the streets toward the place appointed, his hand lay on the hilt of a revolver in the outside pocket of his overcoat. He was a man who would neither seek trouble nor let it overwhelm him. If his life were attempted, he meant to defend it to the last.

He followed side streets purposely, and his footsteps echoed along the deserted road. He knew he was being dogged, for once, when he glanced back, he caught sight of a skulking figure edging along close to a wall. The sight of the spy stirred his blood. Grimly he laughed to himself. They might murder him for what he was doing, but not in time to save the exposure which would be brought to light on the morrow.

The committee met at a road-house near the outskirts of the city, but only long enough to hear Yesler's facts and to appoint another meeting for three hours later at the offices of Eaton. For the committee had come here for secrecy, and they knew that it would be only a short time before Pelton's heelers would be down upon them in force. It was agreed they should divide and slip quietly back to town, wait until everything was quiet and convene again. Meanwhile Eaton would make arrangements to see that his offices would be sufficiently guarded for protection against any attack.

Yesler walked back to town and was within a couple of

blocks of his hotel when he glimpsed two figures crouching against the fence of the alley. He stopped in his tracks, watched them intently an instant, and was startled by a whistle from the rear. He knew at once his retreat, too, was cut off, and without hesitation vaulted the fence in front of a big gray stone house he was passing. A revolver flashed from the alley, and he laughed with a strange kind of delight. His thought was to escape round the house, but trellis work barred the way, and he could not open the gate.

"Trapped, by Jove," he told himself coolly as a bullet struck the trellis close to his head.

He turned back, ran up the steps of the porch and found momentary safety in the darkness of its heavy vines. But this he knew could not last. Running figures were converging toward him at a focal point. He could hear oaths and cries. Some one was throwing aimless shots from a revolver at the porch.

He heard a window go up in the second story and a woman's frightened voice ask. "What is it? Who is there?"

"Let me in. I'm ambushed by thugs," he called back.

"There he is—in the doorway," a voice cried out of the night, and it was followed by a spatter of bullets about him.

He fired at a man leaping the fence. The fellow tumbled back with a kind of scream.

"God! I'm hit."

He could hear steps coming down the stairway and fingers fumbling at the key of the door. His attackers were gathering for a rush, and he wondered whether the rescue was to be too late. They came together, the opening door and the forward pour of huddled figures. He stepped back into the hall.

There was a raucous curse, a shot, and Yesler had slammed the door shut. He was alone in the darkness with his rescuer.

"We must get out of here. They're firing through the door," he said, and "Yes" came faintly back to him from across the hall.

"Do you know where the switch is?" he asked, wondering whether she was going to be such an idiot as to faint at this inopportune moment.

His answer came in a flood of light, and showed him a young woman crouched on the hall-rack a dozen feet from the switch. She was very white, and there was a little stain of crimson on the white lace of her sleeve.

A voice from the landing above demanded quickly, "Who are you, sir?" and after he had looked up', cried in surprise, "Mr. Yesler."

"Miss Balfour," he replied. "I'll explain later. I'm afraid the lady has been hit by a bullet."

He was already beside his rescuer. She looked at him with a trace of a tired smile and said:

"In my arm."

After which she fainted. He picked up the young woman, carried her to the stairs, and mounted them.

"This way," said Virginia, leading him into a bedroom, the door of which was open.

He observed with surprise that she, too, was dressed in evening clothes, and rightly surmised that they had just come back from some social function.

"Is it serious?" asked Virginia, when he had laid his burden on the bed.

She was already clipping with a pair of scissors the sleeve from round the wound.

"It ought not to be," he said after he had examined it. "The bullet has scorched along the fleshy part of the forearm. We must telephone for a doctor at once."

She did so, then found water and cotton for bandages, and helped him make a temporary dressing. The patient recovered consciousness under the touch of the cold water, and asked: what was the matter.

"You have been hurt a little, but not badly I think. Don't you remember? You came down and opened the door to let me in."

"They were shooting at you. What for?" she wanted to know.

He smiled. "Don't worry about that. It's all over with. I'm sorry you were hurt in saving me," said Yesler gently.

"Did I save you?" The gray eyes showed a gleam of pleasure.

"You certainly did."

"This is Mr. Yesler, Laska. Mr. Yesler—Miss Lowe. I think you have never met."

"Never before to-night," he said, pinning the bandage in

place round the plump arm. "There. That's all just now, ma'am. Did I hurt you very much?"

The young woman felt oddly exhilarated. "Not much. I'll forgive you if you'll tell me all about the affair. Why did they want to hurt you?"

His big heart felt very tender toward this girl who had been wounded for him, but he showed it only by a smiling deference.

"You're right persistent, ma'am. You hadn't ought to be bothering your head about any such thing, but if you feel that way I'll be glad to tell you."

He did. While they sat there and waited for the coming of the doctor, he told her the whole story of his attempt to stop the corruption that was eating like a canker at the life of the State. He was a plain man, not in the least eloquent, and he told his story without any sense that he had played any unusual part. In fact, he was ashamed that he had been forced to assume a role which necessitated a kind of treachery to those who thought they had bought him.

Laska Lowe's eyes shone with the delight his tale inspired in her. She lived largely in the land of ideals, and this fight against wrong moved her mightily. She could feel for him none of the shame which he felt for himself at being mixed up in so bad a business. He was playing a man's part, had chosen it at risk of his life. That was enough. In every fiber of her, she was glad that good fortune had given her the chance to bear a part of the battle. In her inmost heart she was even glad that to the day of her death she must bear the scar that would remind her she had suffered in so good a cause.

Virginia, for once obliterating herself, perceived how greatly taken they were with each other. At bottom, nearly every woman is a match-maker. This one was no exception. She liked both this man and this woman, and her fancy had already begun to follow her hopes. Never before had Laska appeared to show much interest in any of the opposite sex with whom her friend had seen her. Now she was all enthusiasm, had forgotten completely the pain of her wound in the spirit's glow.

"She loved me for the danger I had pass'd,
And I loved her that she did pity them.
This only is the witchcraft I have us'd.'"

Virginia quoted softly to herself, her eyes on the young woman so finely unconscious of the emotion that thrilled her.

Not until the clock in the hall below struck two did Yesler remember his appointment in the Ridgway Building. The doctor had come and was about to go. He suggested that if Yesler felt it would be safe for him to go, they might walk across to the hotel together.

"And leave us alone." Laska could have bitten her tongue after the words were out.

Virginia explained. "The Leighs are out of the city to-night, and it happens that even the servants are gone. I asked Miss Lowe to stay with me all night, but, of course, she feels feverish and nervous after this excitement. Couldn't you send a man to watch the rest of the night out in the house?"

"Why don't You stay, Mr. Yesler?" the doctor suggested. "You could sleep here, no doubt."

"You might have your meeting here. It is neutral ground. I can phone to Mr. Ridgway," proposed Virginia in a low voice to Yesler.

"Doesn't that seem to imply that I'm afraid to leave?" laughed Yesler.

"It implies that we are afraid to have you. Laska would worry both on your account and our own. I think you owe it to her to stay."

"Oh, if that's the way it strikes you," he agreed. "Fact is, I don't quite like to leave you anyhow. We'll take Leigh's study. I don't think we shall disturb you at all."

"I'm sure you won't—and before you go, you'll let us know what you have decided to do."

"We shall not be through before morning. You'll be asleep by then," he made answer.

"No, I couldn't sleep till I know all about it."

"Nor I," agreed Laska. "I want to know all about everything."

"My dear young lady, you are to take the sleeping-powders and get a good rest," the doctor demurred. "All about everything is too large an order for your good just now."

Virginia nodded in a businesslike way. "Yes, you're to go to sleep, Laska, and when you waken I'll tell you all about it."

"That would be better," smiled Yesler, and Virginia thought it significant that her friend made no further protest.

Gray streaks began to show in the sky before Yesler tapped

on the door of Virginia's room. She had discarded the rather elaborate evening gown he had last seen her in, and was wearing some soft fabric which hung from the shoulders in straight lines, and defined the figure while lending the effect of a loose and flowing drapery.

"How is your patient?" he asked.

"She has dropped into a good sleep," the girl whispered. "I am sure we don't need to worry about her at all."

"Nevertheless, it's a luxury I'm going to permit myself for a day or two," he smiled. "I don't have my life saved by a young lady very often."

"I'm sure you will enjoy worrying about her," she laughed.

He got back at her promptly. "There's somebody down-stairs worrying about you. He wants to know if there is anything he can do for you, and suggests inviting himself for breakfast in order to make sure."

"Mr. Ridgway?"

"How did you guess it first crack? Mr. Ridgway it is."

She considered a moment. "Yes, tell him to stay. Molly will be back in time to make breakfast, and I want to talk to him. Now tell me what you did."

"We did Mr. Warner. At least I hope so," he chuckled.

"I'm so glad. And who is to be senator? Is it Waring?"

"No. It wouldn't have been possible to elect him even if we had wanted to."

"And you didn't want to," she flashed.

"No, we didn't," he admitted frankly. "We couldn't afford to have it generally understood that this was merely a partisan fight on the Consolidated, and that we were pulling Waring's chestnuts out of the fire for him."

He did not add, though he might have, that Ridgway was tarred with the same brush as the enemy in this matter.

"Then who is it to be?"

"That's a secret. I can't tell even you that. But we have agreed on a man. Waring is to withdraw and throw his influence for him. The Democratic minority will swing in line for him, and we'll do the rest. That's the plan. It may not go through, however."

"I don't see who it can be that you all unite on. Of course, it isn't Mr. Pelton?"

"I should hope not."

"Or Mr. Samuel Yesler?"

"You've used up all the guesses allowed you. If you want to know, why don't you attend the joint session to-day? It ought to be highly interesting."

"I shall," she announced promptly. "And I'll bring Laska with me."

"She won't be able to come."

"I think she will. It's only a scratch."

"I don't like to think how much worse it might have been."

"Then don't think of it. Tell Waring I'll be down presently."

He went down-stairs again, and Miss Balfour returned to the room.

"Was that Mr. Yesler?" quietly asked a voice from the bed.

"Yes, dear. He has gone back to the hotel. He asked about you, of course."

"He is very kind."

"It was thoughtful, since you only saved his life," admitted the ironical Miss Balfour.

"Wasn't it fortunate that we were up?"

"Very fortunate for him that you were."

Virginia crossed the room to the bed and kissed her friend with some subtle significance too elusive for words. Laska appeared, however to appreciate it. At least, she blushed.

CHAPTER 16

AN EXPLOSION IN THE TAURUS

The change of the relationship between Ridgway and his betrothed, brought about by the advent of a third person into his life, showed itself in the manner of their greeting. She had always been chary of lovers' demonstrations, but until his return from Alpine he had been wont to exact his privilege in spite of her reluctance. Now he was content with the hand she offered him.

"You've had a strenuous night of it," he said, after a glance at the rather wan face she offered the new day.

"Yes, we have—and for that matter, I suppose you have, too."

Man of iron that he was, he looked fresh as morning dew. With his usual lack of self-consciousness, he had appropriated Leigh's private bath, and was glowing from contact with ice-cold water and a crash towel.

"We've been making history," he agreed. "How's your friend?"

"She has no fever at all. It was only a scratch. She will be down to breakfast in a minute."

"Good. She must be a thoroughbred to come running down into the bullets for a stranger she has never seen."

"She is. You'll like Laska."

"I'm glad she saved Sam from being made a colander. I can't help liking him, though he doesn't approve of me very much."

"I suppose not."

"He is friendly, too." Ridgway laughed as he recalled their battle over who should be the nominee. "But his conscience rules him. It's a free and liberal conscience, generally speaking—nothing Puritan about it, but a distinctive product of the West. Yet, he would not have me for senator at any price."

"Why?"

"Didn't think I was fit to represent the people; said if I went in, it would be to use the office for my personal profit."

"Wasn't he right?"

"More or less. If I were elected, I would build up my machine, of course, but I would see the people got a show, too."

She nodded agreement. "I don't think you would make a bad senator."

"I would be a live wire, anyhow. Sam had other objections to me. He thought I had been using too much money in this campaign."

"And have you?" she asked, curious to see how he would defend himself.

"Yes. I had to if I were going to stand any chance. It wasn't from choice. I didn't really want to be senator. I can't afford to give the time to it, but I couldn't afford to let Harley name the man either. I was between the devil and the deep sea."

"Then, really, Mr. Yesler came to your rescue."

"That's about it, though he didn't intend it that way."

"And who is to be the senator?"

He gave her a cynical smile. "Warner."

"But I thought—why, surely he—" The surprise of his cool announcement took her breath away.

"No, he isn't the man our combination decided on, but the trouble is that our combination is going to fall through. Sam's an optimist, but you'll see I'm right. There are too many conflicting elements of us in one boat. We can't lose three votes and win, and it's a safe bet we lose them. The Consolidated must know by this time what we have been about all night. They're busy now sapping at our weak links. Our only chance is to win on the first vote, and I am very sure we won't be able to do it."

"Oh, I hope you are not right." A young woman was standing in the doorway, her arm in a sling. She had come in time to hear his prophesy, and in the disappointment of it had forgotten that he was a stranger.

Virginia remedied this, and they went in to breakfast. Laska was full of interest, and poured out eager questions at

Ridgway. It was not for several minutes that Virginia recollected to ask again who was the man they had decided upon.

Her betrothed found some inner source of pleasure that brought out a sardonic smile. "He's a slap in the face at both Harley and me."

"I can't think who—is he honest?"

"As the day."

"And capable?"

"Oh, yes. He's competent enough."

"Presentable?"

"Yes. He'll do the State credit, or rather he would if he were going to be elected."

"Then I give it up."

He was leaning forward to tell, when the sharp buzz of the electric door-bell, continued and sustained, diverted the attention of all of them.

Ridgway put down his napkin. "Probably some one to see me."

He had risen to his feet when the maid opened the door of the dining-room.

"A gentleman to see Mr. Ridgway. He says it is very important."

From the dining-room they could hear the murmur of quick voices, and soon Ridgway returned. He was a transformed man. His eyes were hard as diamonds, and there was the bulldog look of the fighter about his mouth and chin.

"What is it, Waring?" cried Virginia.

"Trouble in the mines. An hour ago Harley's men rushed the Taurus and the New York, and drove my men out. One of my shift-foremen and two of his drillers were killed by an explosion set off by Mike Donleavy, a foreman in the Copper King."

"Did they mean to kill them?" asked the girl whitely.

"I suppose not. But they took the chance. It's murder just the same—by Jove, it's a club with which to beat the legislators into line."

He stopped, his brain busy solving the problem as to how he might best turn this development to his own advantage. Part of his equipment was his ability to decide swiftly and surely issues as they came to him. Now he strode to the telephone and began massing his forces.

"Main 234—Yes—Yes—This the Sun?—

Give me Brayton—Hello, Brayton. Get out a special edition at once charging Harley with murder. Run the word as a red headline clear across the page. Show that Vance Edwards and the other boys were killed while on duty by an attack ordered by Harley. Point out that this is the logical result of his course. Don't mince words. Give it him right from the shoulder. Rush it, and be sure a copy of the paper is on the desk of every legislator before the session opens this morning. Have a reliable man there to see that every man gets one. Scatter the paper broadcast among the miners, too. This is important."

He hung up the receiver, took it down again, and called up Eaton.

"Hello! This you, Steve? Send for Trelawney and Straus right away. Get them to call a mass meeting of the unions for ten o'clock at the courthouse square. Have dodgers printed and distributed announcing it. Shut down all our mines so that the men can come. I want Straus and Trelawney and two or three of the other prominent labor leaders to denounce Harley and lay the responsibility for this thing right at his door. I'll be up there and outline what they had better say."

He turned briskly round to the young women, his eyes shining with a hard bright light. "I'm sorry, but I have got to cut out breakfast this morning. Business is piling up on me too fast. If you'll excuse me, I'll go now."

"What are you going to do?" asked Virginia.

"I haven't time to tell you now. Just watch my smoke," he laughed without mirth.

No sooner did the news of the tragedy reach Simon Harley than he knew the mistake of his subordinates would be a costly one. The foreman, Donleavy, who had directed the attack on the Taurus, had to be brought from the shafthouse under the protection of a score of Pinkerton detectives to safeguard him from the swift vengeance of the miners, who needed but a word to fling themselves against the cordon of police. Harley himself kept his apartments, the hotel being heavily patrolled by guards on the lookout for suspicious characters. The current of public opinion, never in his favor, now ran swiftly against him, and threats were made openly by the infuriated miners to kill him on sight.

The members of the unions came to the massmeeting reading the story of the tragedy as the Sun colored the affair. They stayed sullenly to listen to red-hot speeches against the leader of the trust, and gradually the wrath which was simmering in them began to boil. Ridgway, always with a keen sense of the psychological moment, descended the court-house steps just as this fury was at its height. There were instant cries for a speech from him so persistent that he yielded, though apparently with reluctance. His fine presence and strong deep voice soon gave him the ears of all that dense throng. He was far out of the ordinary as a public speaker, and within a few minutes he had his audience with him. He deprecated any violence; spoke strongly for letting the law take its course; and dropped a suggestion that they send a committee to the State-house to urge that Harley's candidate be defeated for the senatorship.

Like wild-fire this hint spread. Here was something tangible they could do that was still within the law. Harley had set his mind on electing Warner. They would go up there in a body and defeat his plans. Marshals and leaders of companies were appointed. They fell into ranks by fours, nearly ten thousand of them all told. The big clock in the court-house was striking twelve when they began their march to the Statehouse.

William MacLeod Raine

CHAPTER 17

THE ELECTION

At the very moment that the tramp of twenty thousand feet turned toward the State-house, the report of the bribery investigating committee was being read to the legislature met in joint session. The committee reported that it had examined seven witnesses, Yesler, Roper, Landor, James, Reedy, Kellor, and Ward, and that each of then had testified that former Congressman Pelton or others had approached him on behalf of Warner; that an agreement had been made by which the eight votes being cast for Bascom would be give to Warner in consideration of $300,000 in cash, to be held in escrow by Yesler, and that the committee now had the said package, supposed to contain the bills for that amount, in its possession, and was prepared to turn it over to the legislature for examination.

Except for the clerk's voice, as he read the report, a dead silence lay tensely over the crowded hall. Men dared not look at their neighbors, scarce dared breathe, for the terror that hung heavy on their hearts. Scores were there who expected their guilt to be blazoned forth for all the world to read. They waited whitely as the monotonous voice of the clerk went from paragraph to paragraph, and when at last he sat down, having named only the bribers and not the receivers of bribes, a long deep sigh of relief swept the house. Fear still racked them, but for the moment they were safe. Furtively their glances began to go from one to another of their neighbors and ask for how long safety would endure.

One could have heard the rustle of a leaf as the chairman of the committee stepped forward and laid on the desk of the presiding officer the incriminating parcel. It seemed an age while the chief clerk opened it, counted the bills, and announced that one hundred thousand dollars was the sum contained within.

Stephen Eaton then rose in his seat and presented quietly his resolution, that since the evidence submitted was sufficient to convict of bribery, the judge of the district court of the County of Mesa be requested to call a special session of the grand jury to investigate the report. It was not until Sam Yesler rose to speak upon that report that the pent-up storm broke loose.

He stood there in the careless garb of the cattleman, a strong clean-cut figure as one would see in a day's ride, facing with unflinching steel-blue eyes the tempest of human passion he had evoked. The babel of voices rose and fell and rose again before he could find a chance to make himself heard. In the gallery two quietly dressed young, women, one of them with her arm in a sling, leaned forward breathlessly and waited Laska's eyes glowed with deep fire. She was living her hour of hours, and the man who stood with such quiet courage the focus of that roar of rage was the hero of it.

"You call me Judas, and I ask you what Christ I have betrayed. You call me traitor, but traitor to what? Like you, I am under oath to receive no compensation for my services here other than that allowed by law. To that oath I have been true. Have you?

William MacLeod Raine

"For many weeks we have been living in a carnival of bribery, in a debauched hysteria of money-madness. The souls of men have been sifted as by fire. We have all been part and parcel of a man-hunt, an eager, furious, persistent hunt that has relaxed neither night nor day. The lure of gold has been before us every waking hour, and has pursued us into our dreams. The temptation has been ever-present. To some it has been irresistible, to some maddening, to others, thank God! it has but proved their strength. Our hopes, our fears, our loves, our hates: these seducers of honor have pandered to them all. Our debts and our business, our families and our friendships, have all been used to hound us. To-day I put the stigma for this shame where it belongs— upon Simon Harley, head of the Consolidated and a score of other trusts, and upon Waring Ridgway, head of the Mesa Ore-producing Company. These are the debauchers of our commonwealth's fair name, and you, alas! the traffickers who hope to live upon its virtue. I call upon you to-day to pass this resolution and to elect a man to the United States senate who shall owe no allegiance to any power except the people, or to receive forever the brand of public condem- nation. Are you free men? Or do you wear the collar of the Consolidated, the yoke of Waring Ridgway? The vote which you will cast to-day is an answer that shall go flying to the farthest corner of your world, an answer you can never hope to change so long as you live."

He sat down in a dead silence. Again men drew counsel from their fears. The resolution passed unanimously, for none dared vote against it lest he brand himself as bought and sold.

It was in this moment, while the hearts of the guilty were like water, that there came from the lawn outside the roar of a multitude of voices. Swiftly the word passed that ten thousand miner had come to see that Warner was not elected.

That they were in a dangerous frame of mind, all knew. It was a passionate undisciplined mob and to thwart them would have been to invite a riot.

Under these circumstances the joint assembly proceeded to ballot for a senator. The first name called was that of Adams. He was an old cattleman and a Democrat.

"Before voting, I want to resign my plate a few moments to Mr. Landor, of Kit Carson County," he said.

Landor was recognized, a big broad-shouldered plainsman with a leathery face as honest as the sun. He was known and liked by everybody, even by those opposed to him.

"I'm going to make a speech," he announced with the broad smile that showed a flash of white teeth. "I reckon it'll be the first I ever made here, and I promise it will be the last, boys. But I won't keep you long, either. You all know how things have been going; how men have been moving in and out and buying men here like as if they were cattle on the hoof. You've seen it, and I've seen it. But we didn't have the nerve to say it should stop. One man did. He's the biggest man in this big State to-day, and it ain't been five minutes since I heard you holler your lungs out cursing him. You know who I mean—Sam Yesler."

He waited till the renewed storm of cheers and hisses had died away.

"It don't do him any harm for you to holler at him, boys—not a mite. I want to say to you that he's a man. He saw our old friends falling by the wayside and some of you poor weaklings selling yourselves for dollars. Because he is an honest, game man, he set out to straighten things up. I want to tell you that my hat's off to Sam Yesler.

William MacLeod Raine

"But that ain't what I rose for. I'm going to name for the United States senate a clean man, one who doesn't wear either the Harley or the Ridgway brand. He's as straight as a string, not a crooked hair in his head, and every manjack of you knows it. I'm going to name a man"—he stopped an instant to smile genially around upon the circle of uplifted faces—"who isn't any friend of either one faction or another, a man who has just had independence enough to quit a big job because it wasn't on the square. That man's name is Lyndon Hobart. If you want to do yourselves proud, gentlemen, you'll certainly elect him."

If it was a sensation he had wanted to create, he had it. The Warner forces were taken with dumb surprise. But many of them were already swiftly thinking it would be the best way out of a bad business. He would be conservative, as fair to the Consolidated as to the enemy. More, just now his election would appeal to the angry mob howling outside the building, for they could ask nothing more than the election of the man who had resigned rather than order the attack on the Taurus, which had resulted in the death of some of their number.

Hoyle, of the Democrats, seconded the nomination, as also did Eaton, in a speech wherein he defended the course of Ridgway and withdrew his name.

Within a few minutes of the time that Eaton sat down, the roll had been called and Hobart elected by a vote of seventy-three to twenty-four, the others refusing to cast a ballot.

The two young women, sitting together in the front row of the gallery, were glowing with triumphant happiness. Virginia was still clapping her hands when a voice behind her suggested that the circumstances did not warrant her being so happy over the result. She turned, to see Waring

Ridgway smiling down at her.

"But I can't help being pleased. Wasn't Mr. Yesler magnificent?"

"Sam was all right, though he might have eased up a bit when he pitched into me."

"He had to do that to be fair. Everybody knows you and he are friends. I think it was fine of him not to let that make any difference in his telling the truth."

"Oh, I knew it would please you," her betrothed laughed. "What do you say to going out to lunch with me? I'll get Sam, too, if I can."

The young women consulted eyes and agreed very readily. Both of them enjoyed being so near to the heart of things.

"If Mr. Yesler will lunch with the debaucher of the commonwealth, we shall be very happy to join the party," said Virginia demurely.

Ridgway led them down to the floor of the House. Through the dense throng they made their way slowly toward him, Ridgway clearing a path with his broad shoulders.

Suddenly they heard him call sharply, "Look out, Sam."

The explosion of a revolver followed sharply his words. Ridgway dived through the press, tossing men to right and left of him as a steamyacht does the waves. Through the open lane he left in his wake, the young women caught the meaning of the turmoil: the crumpled figure was Yesler swaying into the arms of his friend, Roper, the furious drink-flushed face of Pelton and the menace of the weapon poised for a second shot, the swift impact of Waring's body, and the blow which sent the next bullet crashing into the chandelier overhead. All this they glimpsed momentarily before the press closed in on the tragic scene and cut off their view.

CHAPTER 18

FURTHER DEVELOPMENTS

While Harley had been in no way responsible for Pelton's murderous attack upon Yesler, public opinion held him to account. The Pinkertons who had, up till this time, been employed at the mines, were now moved to the hotel to be ready for an emergency. A special train was held in readiness to take the New Yorker out of the State in the event that the stockman should die. Meanwhile, the harassing attacks of Ridgway continued. Through another judge than Purcell, the absurd injunction against working the Diamond King, the Mary K, and the Marcus Daly had been dissolved, but even this advantage had been neutralized by the necessity of giving back to the enemy the Taurus and the New York, of which he had just possessed himself. All his life he had kept a wheather-eye upon the impulsive and fickle public. There were times when its feeling could be abused with impunity, and other times when this must be respected. Reluctantly, Harley gave the word for the withdrawal of his men from the territory gained. Ridgway pushed his advantage home and secured an injunction, not only against the working, but against the inspection of the Copper King and the Jim Hill. The result of the Consolidated move had been in effect to turn over, temporarily, its two rich mines to be looted by the pirate, and to make him very much stronger than before with his allies, the unions. By his own imprudence, Harley had made a bad situation worse, and delivered himself, with his hands tied, into the power of the enemy.

In the days of turmoil that followed, Waring Ridgway's telling blows scored once and again. The morning after the explosion, he started a relief fund in his paper, the Sun, for the families of the dead miners, contributing two thousand dollars himself. He also insisted that the Consolidated pay damages to the bereaved families to the extent of twenty thousand dollars for each man killed. The town rang with his praises. Mesa had always been proud of his success; had liked the democratic spirit of him that led him to mix on apparently equal terms with his working men, and had backed him in his opposition to the trust because his plucky and unscrupulous fight had been, in a measure, its fight. But now it idolized him. He was the buffer between it and the trust, fighting the battles of labor against the great octopus of Broadway, and beating it to a standstill. He was the Moses destined to lead the working man out of the Egypt of his discontent. Had he not maintained the standard of wages and forced the Consolidated to do the same? Had he not declared an eight-hour day, and was not the trust almost ready to do this also, forced by the impetus his example had given the unions? So Ridgway's agents whispered, and the union leaders, whom he had bought, took up the burden of their tale and preached it both in private talk and in their speeches.

In an attempt to stem the rising tide of denunciation that was spreading from Mesa to the country at large, Harley announced an eight hour day and an immense banquet to all the Consolidated employees in celebration of the occasion. Ten thousand men sat down to the long tables, but when one of the speakers injudiciously mentioned the name of Ridgway, there was steady cheering for ten minutes. It was quite plain that the miners gave him the credit for having forced the Consolidated to the eight-hour day.

The verdict of the coroner's jury was that Vance Edwards and the other deceased miners had come to their death at the hands of the foreman, Michael Donleavy, at the instigation of Simon Harley. True bills were at once drawn up by the prosecuting attorney of Mesa County, an official elected by Ridgway, charging Harley and Donleavy with conspiracy, resulting in the murder of Vance Edwards. The billionaire furnished bail for himself and foreman, treating the indictments merely as part of the attacks of the enemy.

The tragedy in the Taurus brought to the surface a bitterness that had hitherto not been apparent in the contest between the rival copper interests. The lines of division became more sharply drawn, and every business man in Mesa was forced to declare himself on one side or the other. Harley scattered detectives broadcast and imported five hundred Pinkertons to meet any emergency that might arise. The spies of the Consolidated were everywhere, gathering evidence against the Mesa Ore-producing Company, its conduct of the senatorial campaign, its judges, and its supporters Criminal indictments flew back and forth thick as snowflakes in a Christmas storm.

It began to be noticed that an occasional foreman, superintendent, or mining engineer was slipping from the employ of Ridgway to that of the trust, carrying secrets and evidence that would be invaluable later in the courts. Everywhere the money of the Consolidated, scattered lavishly where it would do the most good, attempted to sap the loyalty of the followers of the other candidates. Even Eaton was approached with the offer of a bribe.

But Ridgway's potent personality had built up an esprit de corps not easily to be broken. The adventurers gathered to his side were, for the most part, bound to him by ties personal in their nature. They were financial fillibusters, pledged to stand or fall together, with an interest in their predatory leader's success that was not entirely measurable in dollars and cents. Nor was that leader the man to allow the organization he had builded with such care to become disintegrated while he slept. His alert eye and cheery smile were everywhere, instilling confidence in such as faltered, and dread in those contemplating defection.

He harassed his rival with an audacity that was almost devilish in its unexpected ingenuity. For the first time in his life Simon Harley, the town back on the defensive by a combination of circumstances engineered by a master brain, knew what it was to be checkmated. He had hot the least doubt of ultimate victory, but the tentative success of the brazen young adventurer, were gall and wormwood to his soul. He had made money his god, had always believed it would buy anything worth while except life, but this Western buccaneer had taught him it could not purchase the love of a woman nor the immediate defeat of a man so well armed as Waring Ridgway. In truth, though Harley stuck at nothing, his success in accomplishing the destruction of this thorn in his side was no more appreciable than had been that of Hobart. The Westerner held his own and more, the while he robbed the great trust of its ore under cover of the courts.

In the flush of success, Ridgway, through his lieutenant, Eaton, came to Judge Purcell asking that a receiver be appointed for the Consolidated Supply Company, a subsidiary branch of the trust, on the ground that its affairs were not being properly administered. The Supply Company had paid dividends ranging from fifteen to twenty-five per cent for many years, but Ridgway exercised his right as a stockholder to ask for a receivership. In point of fact, he owned, in the name of Eaton, only one-tenth of one per cent of the stock, but it was enough to serve. For Purcell was a bigoted old Missourian, as courageous and obstinate as perfect health and ignorance could make him. He was quite innocent of any legal knowledge, his own rule of law being to hit a Consolidated head whenever he saw one. Lawyers might argue themselves black in the face without affecting his serenity or his justice.

Purcell granted the application, as well as a restraining order against the payment of dividends until further notice, and appointed Eaton receiver over the protests of the Consolidated lawyers.

Ridgway and Eaton left the court-room together, jubilant over their success. They dined at a restaurant, and spent the evening at the ore-producing company's offices, discussing ways and means. When they had finished, his chief followed Eaton to the doors, an arm thrown affectionately round his shoulder.

"Steve, we're going to make a big killing. I was never so sure of anything in my life as that we shall beat Simon Harley at his own game. We're bound to win. We've got to win."

"I wish I were as sure as you."

"It's hard pounding does it, my boy. We'll drive him out of the Montana copper-fields yet. We'll show him there is one little corner of the U. S. where Simon Harley's orders don't go as the last word."

"He has a hundred dollars to your one."

"And I have youth and mining experience and the inside track, as well as stancher friends than he ever dreamed of," laughed Ridgway, clapping the other on the back. "Well, good night, Steve. Pleasant dreams, old man."

The boyish secretary shook hands warmly. "You're a MAN, chief. If anybody can pull us through it will be you."

Triumphant confidence rang in the other's answering laugh. "You bet I can, Steve,"

CHAPTER 19

ONE MILLION DOLLARS

Eaton, standing on the street curb at the corner of the Ridgway Building, lit a cigar while he hesitated between his rooms and the club. He decided for the latter, and was just turning up the hill, when a hand covered his mouth and an arm was flung around his neck in a stranglehold. He felt himself lifted like a child, and presently discovered that he was being whirled along the street in a closed carriage.

"You needn't be alarmed, Mr. Eaton. We're not going to injure you in the least," a low voice explained in his ear. "If you'll give me your word not to cry out, I'll release your throat."

Eaton nodded a promise, and, when he could find his voice, demanded: "Where are you taking me?"

"You'll see in a minute, sir. It's all right."

The carriage turned into an alley and stopped. Eaton was led to a ladder that hung suspended from the fire-escape, and was bidden to mount. He did so, following his guide to the second story, and being in turn followed by the other man. He was taken along a corridor and into the first of a suite of rooms opening into it. He knew he was in the Mesa House, and suspected at once that he was in the apartments of Simon Harley.

His suspicion ripened to conviction when his captors led him through two more rooms, into one fitted as an office. The billionaire sat at a desk, busy over some legal papers he was reading, but he rose at once and came forward with hand extended to meet Eaton. The young man took his hand mechanically.

"Glad to have the pleasure of talking with, you, Mr. Eaton. You must accept my apologies for my methods of securing a meeting. They are rather primitive, but since you declined to call and see me, I can hold only you to blame." An acid smile touched his lips for a moment, though his eyes were expressionless as a wall. "Mr. Eaton, I have brought you here in this way to have a confidential talk with you, in order that it might not in any way reflect upon you in case we do not come to an arrangement satisfactory to both of us. Your friends cannot justly blame you for this conference, since you could not avoid it. Mr. Eaton, take a chair."

The wills of the two men flashed into each other's eyes like rapiers. The weaker man knew that was before him and braced himself to meet it. He would not sit down. He would not discuss anything. So he told himself once and again to hold himself steady against the impulse to give way to those imperious eyes behind which was the impassive, compelling will.

"Sit down, Mr. Eaton."

"I'll stand, Mr. Harley."

"SIT DOWN."

The cold jade eyes were not to be denied. Eaton's gaze fell sullenly, and he slid into a chair.

"I'll discuss no business except in the presence of Mr. Ridgway," he said doggedly, falling back to his second line of defenses.

"To the contrary, my business is with you and not with Mr. Ridgway."

"I know of no business you can have with me."

"Wherefore I have brought you here to acquaint you with it."

The young man lifted his head reluctantly and waited. If he had been willing to confess it to himself, he feared greatly this ruthless spoiler who had built up the greatest fortune in the world from thousands of wrecked lives. He felt himself choking, just as if those skeleton fingers had been at his throat. but he promised himself ever to yield.

The fathomless, dominant gaze caught and held his eyes. "Mr. Eaton, I came here to crush Ridgway. I am going to stay here till I do. I'm going to wipe him from the map of Montana—ruin him so utterly that he can never recover. It has been my painful duty to do this with a hundred men as strong and as confident as he is. After undertaking such an enterprise, I have never faltered and never relented. The men I have ruined were ruined beyond hope of recovery. None of them have ever struggled to their feet again. I intend to make Waring Ridgway a pauper."

Stephen Eaton could have conceived nothing more merciless than this man's callous pronouncement, than the calm certainty of his unemphasized words. He started to reply, but Harley took the words out of his mouth.

"Don't make a mistake. Don't tie to the paltry successes he has gained. I have not really begun to fight yet."

The young man had nothing to say. His heart was water. He accepted Harley's words as true, for he had told himself the same thing a hundred times. Why had Ridgway rejected the overtures of this colossus of finance? It had been the sheerest folly born of madness to suppose that anybody could stand against him.

"For Ridgway, the die is cast," the iron voice went on. "He is doomed beyond hope. But there is still a chance for you. What do you consider your interest in the Mesa Ore-producing Company worth, Mr. Eaton?"

The sudden question caught Eaton with the force of a surprise. "About three hundred thousand dollars," he heard himself say; and it seemed to him that his voice was speaking the words without his volition.

"I'm going to buy you out for twice that sum. Furthermore, I'm going to take care of your future—going to see that you have a chance to rise."

The waverer's will was in flux, but the loyalty in him still protested. "I can't desert my chief, Mr. Harley."

"Do you call it desertion to leave a raging madman in a sinking boat after you have urged him to seek the safety of another ship?"

"He made me what I am."

"And I will make you ten times what you are. With Ridgway you have no chance to be anything but a subordinate. He is the Mesa Ore-producing Company, and you are merely a cipher. I offer your individuality a chance. I believe in you, and know you to be a strong man." No ironic smile touched Harley's face at this statement. "You need a chance, and I offer it to you. For your own sake take it."

Every grievance Eaton had ever felt against his chief came trooping to his mind. He was domineering. He did ride rough-shod over his allies' opinions and follow the course he had himself mapped out. All the glory of the victory he absorbed as his due. In the popular opinion, Eaton was as a farthing-candle to a great electric search-light in comparison with Ridgway.

"He trusts me," the tempted man urged weakly. He was slipping, and he knew it, even while he assured himself he would never betray his chief.

"He would sell you out to-morrow if it paid him. And what is he but a robber? Every dollar of his holdings is stolen from me. I ask only restitution of you—and I propose to buy at twice, nay at three times, the value of your stolen property. You owe that freebooter no loyalty."

"I can't do it. I can't do it."

"You shall do it." Harley dominated him as bullying schoolmaster does a cringing boy under the lash.

"I can't do it," the young man repeated, all his weak will flung into the denial.

"Would you choose ruin?"

"Perhaps. I don't know," he faltered miserable.

"It's merely a business proposition, young man. The stock

you have to sell is valuable to-day. Reject my offer, and a month from now it will be quoted on the market at half its present figure, and go begging at that. It will be absolutely worthless before I finish. You are not selling out Ridgway. He is a ruined man, anyway. But you—I am going to save you in spite of yourself. I am going to shake you from that robber's clutches."

Eaton got to his feet, pallid and limp as a rag. "Don't tempt me," he cried hoarsely. "I tell you I can't do it, sir."

Harley's cold eye did not release him for an instant. "One million dollars and an assured future, or—absolute, utter ruin, complete and final."

"He would murder me—and he ought to," groaned the writhing victim.

"No fear of that. I'll put you where he can't reach you. Just sign your name to this paper, Mr. Eaton."

"I didn't agree. I didn't say I would."

"Sign here. Or, wait one moment, till I get witnesses." Harley touched a bell, and his secretary appeared in the doorway. "Ask Mr. Mott and young Jarvis to step this way."

Harley held out the pen toward Eaton, looking steadily at him. In a strong man the human eye is a sword among weapons. Eaton quailed. The fingers of the unhappy wretch went out mechanically for the pen. He was sweating terror and remorse, but the essential weakness of the man could not stand out unbacked against the masterful force of this man's imperious will. He wrote his name in the places directed, and flung down the pen like a child in a rage.

"Now get me out of Montana before Ridgway knows," he cried brokenly.

"You may leave to-morrow night, Mr. Eaton. You'll only have to appear in court once personally. We'll arrange it quietly for to-morrow afternoon. Ridgway won't know until it is done and you are gone."

CHAPTER 20

A LITTLE LUNCH AT APHONSE'S

It chanced that Ridgway, through the swinging door of a department store, caught a glimpse of Miss Balfour as he was striding along the street. He bethought him that it was the hour of luncheon, and that she was no end better company than the revamped noon edition of the morning paper. Wherefore he wheeled into the store and interrupted her inspection of gloves.

"I know the bulliest little French restaurant tucked away in a side street just three blocks from here. The happiness disseminated in this world by that chef's salads will some day carry him past St. Peter with no questions asked."

"You believe in salvation by works?" she parried, while she considered his invitation.

"So will you after a trial of Alphonse's salad."

"Am I to understand that I am being invited to a theological discussion of a heavenly salad concocted by Father Alphonse?"

"That is about the specifications."

"Then I accept. For a week my conscience has condemned me for excess of frivolity. You offer me a chance to expiate without discomfort. That is my idea of heaven. I have always believed it a place where one pastures in rich meadows of pleasure, with penalties and consciences all excluded from its domains."

"You should start a church," he laughed. "It would have a great following—especially if you could operate your heaven this side of the Styx."

She found his restaurant all he had claimed, and more. The little corner of old Paris set her eyes shining. The fittings were Parisian to the least detail. Even the waiter spoke no English.

"But I don't see how they make it pay. How did he happen to come here? Are there enough people that appreciate this kind of thing in Mesa to support it?"

He smiled at her enthusiasm. "Hardly. The place has a scarce dozen of regular patrons. Hobart comes here a good deal. So does Eaton. But it doesn't pay financially. You see, I know because I happen to own it. I used to eat at Alphonse's restaurant in Paris. So I sent for him. It doesn't follow that one has to be less a slave to the artificial comforts of a supercivilized world because one lives at Mesa."

"I see it doesn't. You are certainly a wonderful man."

"Name anything you like. I'll warrant Alphonse can make good if it is not outside of his national cuisine," he boasted.

She did not try his capacity to the limit, but the oysters, the salad, the chicken soup were delicious, with the ultimate perfection that comes only out of Gaul.

They made a delightfully gay and intimate hour of it, and were still lingering over their demi-tasse when Yesler's name was mentioned.

"Isn't it splendid that he's doing so well?" cried the girl with enthusiasm. "The doctor says that if the bullet had gone a fraction of an inch lower, he would have died. Most men would have died anyhow, they say. It was his clean outdoor life and magnificent constitution that saved him."

"That's what pulled him through," he nodded. "It would have done his heart good to see how many friends he had. His recovery was a continuous performance ovation. It would have been a poorer world for a lot of people if Sam Yesler had crossed the divide."

"Yes. It would have been a very much poorer one for several I know."

He glanced shrewdly at her. "I've learned to look for a particular application when you wear that particularly sapient air of mystery."

Her laugh admitted his hit. "Well, I was thinking of Laska. I begin to think HER fair prince has come."

"Meaning Yesler?"

"Yes. She hasn't found it out herself yet. She only knows she is tremendously interested."

"He's a prince all right, though he isn't quite a fairy. The woman that gets him will be lucky.

"The man that gets Laska will be more that lucky," she protested loyally.

"I dare say," he agreed carelessly. "But, then, good women are not so rare as good men. There. are still enough of them left to save the world. But when it comes to men like Sam— well, it would take a Diogenes to find another."

"I don't see how even Mr. Pelton, angry as he was, dared shoot him."

"He had been drinking hard for a week. That will explain anything when you add it to his, temperament. I never liked the fellow."

"I suppose that is why you saved his life when the miners took him and were going to lynch him?"

"I would not have lifted a hand for him. That's the bald truth. But I couldn't let the boys spoil the moral effect of their victory by so gross a mistake. It would have been playing right into Harley's hands."

"Can a man get over being drunk in five minutes? I never saw anybody more sober than Mr. Pelton when the mob were crying for vengeance and you were fighting them back."

"A great shock will sober a man. Pelton is an errant coward, and he had pretty good reason to think he had come to the end of the passage. The boys weren't playing. They meant business."

"They would not have listened to another man in the world except you," she told him proudly.

"It was really Sam they listened to—when he sent out the message asking them to let the law have its way."

"No, I think it was the way you handled the message. You're

a wizard at a speech, you know."

"Thanks."

He glanced up, for Alphonse was waiting at his elbow.

"You're wanted on the telephone, monsieur."

"You can't get away from business even for an hour, can you?" she rallied. "My heaven ,wouldn't suit you at all, unless I smuggled in a trust for you to fight."

"I expect it is Eaton," he explained. "Steve phoned down to the office that he isn't feeling well to-day. I asked him to have me called up here. If he isn't better, I'm going to drop round and see him."

But when she caught sight of his face as he returned she knew it was serious.

"What's the matter? Is it Mr. Eaton? Is he very ill?" she cried.

His face was set like broken ice refrozen. "Yes, it's Eaton. They say—but it can't be true!"

She had never seen him so moved. "What is it, Waring?"

"The boy has sold me out. He is at the courthouse now, undoing my work—the Judas!"

The angry blood swept imperiously into her cheeks. "Don't waste any more time with me, Waring. Go—go and save yourself from the traitor. Perhaps it is not too late yet."

He flung her a grateful look. "You're true blue, Virginia. Come! I'll leave you at the store as we pass."

The defection of Eaton bit his chief to the quick. The force of the blow itself was heavy—how heavy he could not tell till he could take stock of the situation. He could see that he would be thrown out of court in the matter of the Consolidated Supply Company receivership, since Eaton's stock would now be in the hands of the enemy. But what was of more importance was the fact that Eaton's interest in the Mesa Ore-producing Company now belonged to Harley, who could work any amount of mischief with it as a lever for litigation.

The effect, too, of the man's desertion upon the morale of the M. O. P. forces must be considered and counteracted, if possible. He fancied he could see his subordinates looking shiftyeyed at each other and wondering who would slip away next.

If it had been anybody but Steve! He would as soon have distrusted his right hand as Steve Eaton. Why, he had made the man, had picked him out when he was a mere clerk, and tied him to himself by a hundred favors. Up on the Snake River he had saved Steve's life once when he was drowning. The boy had always been as close to him as a brother. That Steve should turn traitor was not conceivable. He knew all his intimate plans, stood second to himself in the company. Oh, it was a numbing blow! Ridgway's sense of personal loss and outrage almost obliterated for the moment his appreciation of the business loss.

The motion to revoke the receivership of the Supply Company was being argued when Ridgway entered the court-room. Within a few minutes the news had spread like wild-fire that Eaton was lined up with the Consolidated, and already the paltry dozen of loafers in the court-room had swelled into hundreds, all of them eager for any sensation that might develop.

Ridgway's broad shoulders flung aside the crowd and opened a way to the vacant chair waiting for him. One of his lawyers had the floor and was flaying Eaton with a vitriolic tongue, the while men craned forward all over the room to get a glimpse of the traitor's face.

Eaton sat beside Mott, dry-lipped and pallid, his set eyes staring vacantly into space. Once or twice he flung a furtive glance about him. His stripped and naked soul was enduring a foretaste of the Judgment Day. The whip of scorn with which the lawyer lashed him cut into his shrinking sensibilities, and left him a welter of raw and livid wales. Good God! why had he not known it would be like this? He was paying for his treachery and usury, and it was being burnt into him that as the years passed he must continue to pay in self-contempt and the distrust of his fellows.

The case had come to a hearing before Judge Hughes, who was not one of Ridgway's creatures. That on its merits it would be decided in favor of the Consolidated was a foregone conclusion. It was after the judge had rendered the expected decision that the dramatic moment of the day came to gratify the seasoned court frequenters.

Eaton, trying to slip as quietly as possible from the room, came face to face with his former chief. For an interminable instant the man he had betrayed, blocking the way squarely, held the trembling wretch in the blaze of his scorn. Ridgway's contemptuous eyes sifted to the ingrate's soul until it shriveled. Then he stood disdainfully to one side so that the man might not touch him as he passed.

Some one in the back of the room broke the tense silence and hissed: "The damned Judas!" Instantly echoes of "Judas! Judas!" filled the room, and pursued Eaton to his cab. It would be many years before he could recall without scalding shame that moment when the finger of public scorn was pointed at him in execration.

CHAPTER 21

HARLEY SCORES

What Harley had sought in the subornation of Eaton had been as much the moral effect of his defection as the tangible results themselves. If he could shake the confidence of the city and State in the freebooter's victorious star, he would have done a good day's work. He wanted the impression to spread that Ridgway's success had passed its meridian.

Nor did he fail of his purpose by more than a hair's breadth. The talk of the street saw the beginning of the end. The common voice ran: "It's 'God help Ridgway' now. He's down and out."

But Waring Ridgway was never more dangerous than in apparent defeat. If he were hit hard by Eaton's treachery, no sign of it was apparent in the jaunty insouciance of his manner. Those having business with him expected to find him depressed and worried, but instead met a man the embodiment of vigorous and confident activity. If the subject were broached, he was ready to laugh with them at Eaton's folly in deserting at the hour when victory was assured.

It was fortunate for Ridgway that the county elections came on early in the spring and gave him a chance to show that his power was still intact. He arranged to meet at once the political malcontents of the State who were banded together against the growing influence of the Consolidated. He had a few days before called together representative men from all parts of the State to discuss a program of action against the enemy, and Ridgway gave a dinner for them at the Quartzite, the evening of Eaton's defection.

He was at the critical moment when any obvious irresolution would have been fatal. His allies were ready to concede his defeat if he would let them. But he radiated such an assured atmosphere of power, such an unconquerable current of vigor, that they could not escape his own conviction of unassailability. He was at his genial, indomitable best, the magnetic charm of fellowship putting into eclipse the selfishness of the man. He had been known to boast of his political exploits, of how he had been the Warwick that had made and unmade governors and United States senators; but the fraternal "we" to-night replaced his usual first person singular.

The business interests of the Consolidated were supreme all over the State. That corporation owned forests and mills and railroads and mines. It ran sheep and cattle-ranches as well as stores and manufactories. Most of the newspapers in the State were dominated by it. Of a population of two hundred and fifty thousand, it controlled more than half directly by the simple means of filling dinner-pails. That so powerful a corporation, greedy for power and wealth, should create a strong but scattered hostility in the course of its growth, became inevitable. This enmity Ridgway proposed to consolidate into a political organization, with opposition to the trust as its cohesive principle, that should hold the balance of power in the State.

When he rose to explain his object in calling them together,

Ridgway's clear, strong presentment of the situation, backed by his splendid bulk and powerful personality, always bold and dramatic, shocked dormant antagonisms to activity as a live current does sluggish inertia. For he had eminently the gift of moving speech. The issue was a simple one, he pointed out. Reduced to ultimates, the question was whether the State should control the Consolidated or the Consolidated the State. With simple, telling force he faced the insidious growth of the big copper company, showing how every independent in the State was fighting for his business life against its encroachments, and was bound to lose unless the opposition was a united one. Let the independents obtain and keep control of the State politically and the trust might be curbed; not otherwise. In eternal vigilance and in union lay safety.

He sat down in silence more impressive than any applause. But after the silence came a deluge of cheers, the thunder of them sweeping up and down the long table like a summer storm across a lake.

Presently the flood-gates of talk were unloosed, and the conservatives began to be heard. Opposition was futile because it was too late, they claimed. A young Irishman, primed for the occasion, jumped to his feet with an impassioned harangue that pedestaled Ridgway as the Washington of the West. He showed how one man, in coalition with the labor-unions, had succeeded in carrying the State against the big copper company; how he had elected senators and governors, and legislators and judges. If one man could so cripple the octopus, what could the best blood of the State, standing together, not accomplish? He flung Patrick Henry and Robert Emmet and Daniel Webster at their devoted heads, demanding liberty or death with the bridled eloquence of his race.

But Ridgway was not such a tyro at the game of politics as to depend upon speeches for results. His fine hand had been working quietly for months to bring the malcontents into one camp, shaping every passion to which men are heir to serve his purpose. As he looked down the table he could read in the faces before him hatred, revenge, envy, fear, hope, avarice, recklessness, and even love, as the motives which he must fuse to one common end. His vanity stood on tiptoe at his superb skill in playing on men's wills. He knew he could mold these men to work his desire, and the sequel showed he was right.

When the votes were counted at the end of the bitter campaign that followed, Simon Harley's candidates went down to disastrous defeat all over the State, though he had spent money with a lavish hand. In Mesa County, Ridgway had elected every one of his judges and retired to private life those he could not influence.

Harley's grim lips tightened when the news reached him. "Very well," he said to Mott "We'll see if these patriots can't be reached through their stomachs better than their brains. Order every mill and mine and smelter of the Consolidated closed to-night. Our employees have voted for this man Ridgway. Let him feed them or let them starve."

"But the cost to you—won't it be enormous?" asked Mott, startled at his chief's drastic decision.

Harley bared his fangs with a wolfish smile. "We'll make the public pay. Our store-houses are full of copper. Prices will jump when the supply is reduced fifty per cent. We'll sell at an advance, and clean up a few millions out of the shut-down. Meanwhile we'll starve this patriotic State into submission."

It came to pass even as Harley had predicted. With the

William MacLeod Raine

Consolidated mines closed, copper, jumped up—up—up. The trust could sit still and coin money without turning a hand, while its employees suffered in the long, bitter Northern winter. All the troubles usually pursuant on a long strike began to fall upon the families of the miners.

When a delegation from the miners' union came to discuss the situation with Harley he met them blandly, with many platitudes of sympathy. He regretted—he regretted exceedingly—the necessity that had been forced upon him of closing the mines. He had delayed doing so in the hope that the situation might be relieved. But it had grown worse, until he had been forced to close. No, he was afraid he could not promise to reopen this winter, unless something were done to ameliorate conditions in the court. Work would begin at once, however, if the legislators would pass a bill making it optional with any party to a suit to have the case transferred to another judge in case he believed the bias of the presiding judge would be prejudicial to an impartial hearing.

Ridgway was flung at once upon the defensive. His allies, the working men, demanded of him that his legislature pass the bill wanted by Harley, in order that work might recommence. He evaded their demands by proposing to arbitrate his difficulties with the Consolidated, by offering to pay into the union treasury hall a million dollars to help carry its members through the winter. He argued to the committee that Harley was bluffing, that within a few weeks the mines and smelters would again be running at their full capacity; but when the pressure on the legislators he had elected became so great that he feared they would be swept from their allegiance to him, he was forced to yield to the clamor.

It was a great victory for Harley. Nobody recognized how great a one more accurately than Waring Ridgway. The leader of the octopus had dogged him over the shoulders of the people, had destroyed at a single blow one of his two principal sources of power. He could no longer rely on the courts to support him, regardless of justice.

Very well. If he could not play with cogged dice, he was gambler enough to take the honest chances of the game without flinching. No despair rang in his voice. The look in his eye was still warm and confident. Mesa questioned him with glimpses friendly but critical. They found no fear in his bearing, no hint of doubt in his indomitable assurance.

CHAPTER 22

"NOT GUILTY"—"GUILTY"

Ridgway's answer to the latest move of Simon Harley was to put him on trial for his life to answer the charge of having plotted and instigated the death of Vance Edwards. Not without reason, the defense had asked for a change of venue, alleging the impossibility of securing a fair trial at Mesa. The courts had granted the request and removed the case to Avalanche.

On the second day of the trial Aline sat beside her husband, a dainty little figure of fear, shrinking from the observation focused upon her from all sides. The sight of her forlorn sensitiveness so touched Ridgway's heart that he telegraphed Virginia Balfour to come and help support her through the ordeal.

Virginia came, and henceforth two women, both of them young and unusually attractive, gave countenance to the man being tried for his life. Not that he needed their support for himself, but for the effect they might have on the jury. Harley had shrewdly guessed that the white-faced child he had married, whose pathetic beauty was of so haunting a type, and whose big eyes were so quick to reflect emotions, would be a valuable asset to set against the black-clad widow of Vance Edwards.

For its effect upon himself, so far as the trial was concerned, Simon Harley cared not a whit. He needed no bolstering. The old wrecker carried an iron face to the ordeal. His leathern heart was as foreign to fear as to pity. The trial was an unpleasant bore to him, but nothing worse. He had, of course, cast an anchor of caution to windward by taking care to have the jury fixed. For even though his array of lawyers was a formidably famous one, he was no such child as to trust his case to a Western jury on its merits while the undercurrent of popular opinion was setting so strongly against him. Nor had he neglected to see that the court-room was packed with detectives to safeguard him in the event that the sympathy of the attending miners should at any time become demonstrative against him.

The most irritating feature of the trial to the defendant was the presence of the little woman in black, whose burning eyes never left for long his face. He feigned to be unconscious of her regard, but nobody in the court-room was more sure of that look of enduring, passionate hatred than its victim. He had made her a widow, and her heart cried for revenge. That was the story the eyes told dumbly.

From first to last the case was bitterly contested, and always with the realization among those present—except for that somber figure in black, whose beady eyes gimleted the defendant—that it was another move in the fight between the rival copper kings. The district attorney had worked up his case very carefully, not with much hope of securing a conviction, but to mass a total of evidence that would condemn the Consolidated leader-before the world.

To this end, the foreman, Donleavy, had been driven by a process of sweating to turn State's evidence against his master. His testimony made things look black for Harley, but when Hobart took the stand, a palpably unwilling witness, and supported his evidence, the Ridgway adherents were openly jubilant. The lawyers for the defense made much of the fact that Hobart had just left the Consolidated service after a disagreement with the defendant and had been elected to the senate by his enemies, but the impression made by his moderation and the fine restraint of his manner, combined with his reputation for scrupulous honesty, was not to be shaken by the subtle innuendos and blunt aspersions of the legal array he faced.

Nor did the young district attorney content himself with Hobart's testimony. He put his successor, Mott, on the stand, and gave him a bad hour while he tried to wring the admission out of him that Harley had personally ordered the attack on the miners of the Taurus. But for the almost constant objections of the opposing counsel, which gave him time to recover himself, the prosecuting attorney would have succeeded.

Ridgway, meeting him by chance after luncheon at the foot of the hotel elevator—for in a town the size of Avalanche, Waring had found it necessary to put up at the same hotel as the enemy or take second best, an alternative not to his fastidious taste—rallied him upon the predicament in which he had found himself.

"It's pretty hard to tell the truth, the whole truth, and nothing but the truth, without making indiscreet admissions about one's friends, isn't it?" he asked, with his genial smile.

"Did I make any indiscreet admissions?"

"I don't say you did, though you didn't look as if you were enjoying yourself. I picked up an impression that you had your back to the wall; seemed to me the jury rather sized it up that way, Mott."

"We'll know what the jury thinks in a few days."

"Shall we?" the other laughed aloud. "Now, I'm wondering whether we shall know what they really think."

"If you mean that the jury has been tampered with it is your duty to place your evidence before the court, Mr. Ridgway."

"When I hear the verdict I'll tell you what I think about the jury," returned the president of the Ore-producing Company, with easy impudence as he passed into the elevator.

At the second floor Waring left it and turned toward the ladies' parlor. It had seemed to him that Aline had looked very tired and frail at the morning session, and he wanted to see Virginia about arranging to have them take a long drive into the country that afternoon. He had sent his card up with a penciled note to the effect that he would wait for her in the parlor.

But when he stepped through the double doorway of the ornate room it was to become aware of a prior occupant. She was reclining on a divan at the end of the large public room. Neither lying nor sitting, but propped up among a dozen pillows with head and limbs inert and the long lashes drooped on the white cheeks, Aline looked the pathetic figure of a child fallen asleep from sheer exhaustion after a long strain.

Since he was the man he was, unhampered by any too fine sense of what was fitting, he could no more help approaching than he could help the passionate pulse of pity that stirred in his heart at sight of her forlorn weariness.

William MacLeod Raine

Her eyes opened to find his grave compassion looking down at her. She showed no surprise at his presence, though she had not previously known of it. Nor did she move by even so much as the stir of a limb.

"This is wearing you out," he said, after the long silence in which her gaze was lost helplessly in his. "You must go home—away from it all. You must forget it, and if it ever crosses your mind think of it as something with which you have no concern."

"How can I do that—now."

The last word slipped out not of her will, but from an undisciplined heart. It stood for the whole tangled story of her troubles: the unloved marriage which had bereft her of her heritage of youth and joy, the love that had found her too late and was so poignant a fount of distress to her, the web of untoward circumstance in which she was so inextricably entangled.

"How did you ever come to do it?" he asked roughly, out of the bitter impulse of his heart.

She knew that the harshness was not for her, as surely as she knew what he meant by his words.

"I did wrong. I know that now, but I didn't know it then. Though even then I felt troubled about it. But my guardian said it was best, and I knew so little. Oh, so very, very little. Why was I not taught things, what every girl has a right to know—until life teaches me—too late?"

Nothing he could say would comfort her. For the inexorable facts forbade consolation. She had made shipwreck of her life before the frail raft of her destiny had well pushed forth from harbor. He would have given much to have been able to take the sadness out of her great childeyes, but he knew that not even by the greatness of his desire could he take up her burden. She must carry it alone or sink under it.

"You must go away from here back to your people. If not now, then as soon as the trial is over. Make him take you to your friends for a time."

"I have no friends that can help me." She said it in an even little voice of despair.

"You have many friends. You have made some here. Virginia is one." He would not name himself as only a friend, though he had set his iron will to claim no more.

"Yes, Virginia is my friend. She is good to me. But she is going to marry you, and then you will both forget me."

"I shall never forget you." He cried it in a low, tense voice, his clenched hands thrust into the pockets of his sack coat.

Her wan smile thanked him. It was the most he would let himself say. Though her heart craved more, she knew she must make the most of this.

"I came up to see Virginia," he went on, with a change of manner. "I want her to take you driving this afternoon. Forget about that wretched trial if you can. Nothing of importance will take place to-day."

He turned at the sound of footsteps, and saw that Miss Balfour had come into the room.

"I want you to take Mrs. Harley into the fresh sunshine and clear air this afternoon. I have been telling her to forget this trial. It's a farce, anyhow. Nothing will come of it. Take her out to the Homes—take and cheer her up."

"Yes, my lord." Virginia curtseyed obediently.

"It will do you good, too."

She shot a mocking little smile at him. "It's very good of you to think of me."

"Still, I do sometimes."

"Whenever it is convenient," she added.

But with Aline watching them the spirit of badinage in him was overmatched. He gave it up and asked what kind of a rig he should send round. Virginia furnished him the necessary specifications, and he turned to go.

As he left the room Simon Harley entered. They met face to face, and after an instant's pause each drew aside to allow the other to pass. The New Yorker inclined his head silently and moved forward toward his wife. Ridgway passed down the corridor and into the elevator.

As the days of the trial passed excitement grew more tense. The lawyers for the prosecution and the defense made their speeches to a crowded and enthralled court-room. There was a feverish uncertainty in the air. It reached a climax when the jury stayed out for eleven hours before coming to a verdict. From the moment it filed back into the court-room with solemn faces the dramatic tensity began to foreshadow the tragedy about to be enacted. The woman Harley had made a widow sat erect and rigid in the seat where she had been throughout the trial. Her eyes blazed with a hatred that bordered madness. Ridgway had observed that neither Aline

Harley nor Virginia was present, and a note from the latter had just reached him to the effect that Aline was ill with the strain of the long trial. Afterward Ridgway could never thank his pagan gods enough that she was absent.

There was a moment of tense waiting before the judge asked:

"Gentlemen of the jury, have you reached a verdict?"

The foreman rose. "We have, your honor."

A folded note was handed to the judge. He read it slowly, with an inscrutable face.

"Is this your verdict, gentlemen of the jury?"

"It is, your honor."

Silence, full and rigid, held the room after the words "Not guilty" had fallen from the lips of the judge. The stillness was broken by a shock as of an electric bolt from heaven.

The exploding echoes of a pistol-shot reverberated. Men sprang wildly to their feet, gazing at each other in the distrust that fear generates. But one man was beyond being startled by any more earthly sounds. His head fell forward on the table in front of him, and a thin stream of blood flowed from his lips. It was Simon Harley, found guilty, sentenced, and executed by the judge and jury sitting in the outraged, insane heart of the woman he had made a widow.

Mrs. Edwards had shot him through the head with a revolver she had carried in her shoppingbag to exact vengeance in the event of a miscarriage of justice.

William MacLeod Raine

CHAPTER 23

ALINE TURNS A CORNER

Aline might have been completely prostrated by the news of her husband's sudden end, coming as it did as the culmination of a week of strain and horror. That she did not succumb was due, perhaps, to Ridgway's care for her. When Harley's massive gray head had dropped forward to the table, his enemy's first thought had been of her. As soon as he knew that death was sure, he hurried to the hotel.

He sent his card up, and followed it so immediately that he found her scarcely risen from the divan on which she had been lying in the receiving-room of her apartments. The sleep was not yet shaken from her lids, nor was the wrinkled flush smoothed from the soft cheek that had been next the cushion. Even in his trouble for her he found time to be glad that Virginia was not at the moment with her. It gave him the sense of another bond between them that this tragic hour. should belong to him and her alone—this hour of destiny when their lives swung round a corner beyond which lay wonderful vistas of kindly sunbeat and dewy starlight stretching to the horizon's edge of the long adventure.

She checked the rush of glad joy in her heart the sight of him always brought, and came forward slowly. One glance at his face showed that he had brought grave news.

"What is it? Why are you here?" she cried tensely.

"To bring you trouble, Aline."

"Trouble!" Her hand went to her heart quickly.

"It is about—Mr. Harley."

She questioned him with wide, startled eyes, words hesitating on her trembling lips and flying unvoiced.

"Child—little partner—the orders are to be brave." He came forward and took her hands in his, looking down at her with eyes she thought full of infinitely kind pity.

"Is it—have they—do you mean the verdict?"

"Yes, the verdict; but not the verdict of which you are thinking."

She turned a quivering face to his. "Tell me. I shall be brave."

He told her the brutal fact as gently as he could, while he watched the blood ebb from her face. As she swayed he caught her in his arms and carried her to the divan. When, presently, her eyes fluttered open, it was to look into his pitiful ones. He was kneeling beside her, and her head was pillowed on his arm.

"Say it isn't true," she murmured.

"It is true, dear."

She moved her head restlessly, and he took away his arm, rising to draw a chair close to the lounge. She slipped her two hands under her head, letting them lie palm to palm on the sofapillow. The violet eyes looked past him into space. Her tangled thoughts were in a chaos of disorder. Even though she had known but a few months and loved not at all the grim, gray-haired man she had called husband, the sense of wretched bereavement, the nearness of death, was strong on her. He had been kind to her in his way, and the inevitable closeness of their relationship, repugnant as it had been to her, made its claims felt. An hour ago he had been standing here, the strong and virile ruler over thousands. Now he lay stiff and cold, all his power shorn from him without a second's warning. He had kissed her good-by, solicitous for her welfare, and it had been he that had been in need of care rather than she. Two big tears hung on her lids and splashed to her cheeks. She began to sob, and half-turned on the divan, burying her face in her hands.

Ridgway let her weep without interruption for a time, knowing that it would be a relief to her surcharged heart and overwrought nerves. But when her sobs began to abate she became aware of his hand resting on her shoulder. She sat up, wiping her eyes, and turned to him a face sodden with grief.

"You are good to me," she said simply.

"If my goodness were only less futile! Heaven knows what I would give to ward off trouble from you. But I can't, nor can I bear it for you."

"But it is a help to know you would if you could. He—I think he wanted to ward off grief from me, but he could not, either. I was often lonely and sad, even though he was kind to me. And now he has gone. I wish I had told him how much I appreciated his goodness to me."

"Yes, we all feel that when we have lost some one we love. It is natural to wish we had been better to them and showed them how much we cared. Let me tell you about my mother. I was thirteen when she died. It was in summer. She had not been well for a long time. The boys were going fishing that day and she asked me to stay at home. I had set my heart on going, and I thought it was only a fancy of hers. She did not insist on my staying, so I went, but felt uncomfortable all day. When I came back in the evening they told me she was dead. I felt as if some great icy hand were tightening, on my heart. Somehow I couldn't break down and cry it out. I went around with a white, set face and gave no sign. Even at the funeral it was the same. The neighbors called me hardhearted and pointed me out to their sons as a terrible warning. And all the time I was torn with agony."

"You poor boy."

"And one night she came to me in a dream. She did not look as she had just before she died, but strong and beautiful, with the color in her face she used to have. She smiled at me and kissed me and rumpled my hair as she used to do. I knew, then, it was all right. She understood, and I didn't care whether others did or not. I woke up crying, and after I had had my grief out I was myself again."

"It was so sweet of her to think to come to you. She must have been loving you up in heaven and saw you were troubled, and came down just to comfort you and tell you it was all right," the girl cried with soft sympathy.

"That's how I understood it. Of course, I was only a boy, but somehow I knew it was more than a dream. I'm not a spiritualist. I don't believe such things happen, but I know it happened to me," he finished illogically, with a smile.

She sighed. "He was always so thoughtful of me, too. I do wish I had—could have been—more—"

She broke off without finishing, but he understood.

"You must not blame yourself for that. He would be the first to tell you so. He took you for what you could give him, and these last days were the best he had known for many years."

"He was so good to me. Oh, you don't know how good."

"It was a great pleasure to him to be good to you, the greatest pleasure he knew."

She looked up as he spoke, and saw shining deep in his eyes the spirit that had taught him to read so well the impulse of another lover, and, seeing it, she dropped her eyes quickly in order not to see what was there. With him it had been only an instant's uncontrollable surge of ecstasy. He meant to wait. Every instinct of the decent thing told him not to take advantage of her weakness, her need of love to rest upon in her trouble, her transparent care for him and confidence in him so childlike in its entirety. For convention he did not care a turn of his hand, but he would do nothing that might shock her self-respect when she came to think of it later. Sternly he brought himself back to realities.

"Shall I see Mr. Mott for you and send him here? It would be better that he should make the arrangements than I."

"If you please. I shall not see you again before I go, then?" Her lips trembled as she asked the question.

"I shall come down to the hotel again and see you before you go. And now good-by. Be brave, and don't reproach yourself. Remember that he would not wish it."

The door opened, and Virginia came in, flushed with rapid walking. She had heard the news on the street and had hurried back to the hotel.

Her eyes asked of Ridgway: "Does she know?" and he answered in the affirmative. Straight to Aline she went and wrapped her in her arms, the latent mothering instinct that is in every woman aroused and dormant.

"Oh, my dear, my dear," she cried softly.

Ridgway slipped quietly from the room and left them together.

CHAPTER 24

A GOOD SAMARITAN

Yesler, still moving slowly with a walking stick by reason of his green wound, left the street-car and made his way up Forest Road to the house which bore the number 792. In the remote past there had been some spasmodic attempt to cultivate grass and raise some shade-trees along the side-walks, but this had long since been given up as abortive. An air of decay hung over the street, the unmistakable suggestion of better days. This was writ large over the house in front of which Yesler stopped. The gate hung on one hinge, boards were missing from the walk, and a dilapidated shutter, which had once been green, swayed in the breeze.

A woman of about thirty, dark and pretty but poorly dressed, came to the door in answer to his ring. Two little children, a boy and a girl, with their mother's shy long-lashed Southern eyes of brown, clung to her skirts and gazed at the stranger.

"This is where Mr. Pelton lives, is it not?" he asked.

"Yes, sir."

"Is he at home?"

"Yes, sir."

"May I see him?"

"He's sick."

"I'm sorry to hear it. Too sick to be seen? If not, I should like very much to see him. I have business with him."

The young woman looked at him a little defiantly and a little suspiciously. "Are you a reporter?"

Sam smiled. "No, ma'am."

"Does he owe you money" He could see the underlying blood dye her dusky cheeks when she asked the question desperately, as it seemed to him with a kind of brazen shame to which custom had inured her. She had somehow the air of some gentle little creature of the forests defending her young.

"Not a cent, ma'am. I don't want to do him any harm."

"I didn't hear your name."

"I haven't mentioned it," he admitted, with the sunny smile that was a letter of recommendation in itself. "Fact is I'd rather not tell it till he sees me."

From an adjoining room a querulous voice broke into their conversation. "Who is it, Norma?"

"A gentleman to see you, Tom."

"Who is it?" more sharply.

"It is I, Mr. Pelton. I came to have a talk with you." Yesler pushed forward into the dingy sitting-room with the pertinacity of a bookagent. "I heard you were not well, and I came to find out if I can do anything for you."

The stout man lying on the lounge grew pale before the blood reacted in a purple flush. His very bulk emphasized the shabbiness of the stained and almost buttonless Prince Albert coat he wore, the dinginess of the little room he seemed to dwarf.

"Leave my house, seh. You have ruined this family, and you come to gloat on your handiwork. Take a good look, and then go, Mr. Yesler. You see my wife in cotton rags doing her own work. Is it enough, seh?"

The slim little woman stepped across the room and took her place beside her husband. Her eyes flashed fire at the man she held responsible for the fall of her husband. Yesler's generous heart applauded the loyalty which was proof against both disgrace and poverty. For in the past month both of these had fallen heavily upon her. Tom Pelton had always lived well, and during the past few years he had speculated in ventures far beyond his means. Losses had pursued him, and he had looked to the senatorship to recoup himself and to stand off the creditors pressing hard for payment. Instead he had been exposed, disgraced, and finally disbarred for attempted bribery. Like a horde of hungry rats his creditors had pounced upon the discredited man and wrested from him the remnants of his mortgaged property. He had been forced to move into a mere cottage and was a man without a future. For the only profession at which he had skill enough to make a living was the one from which he had been cast as unfit to practise it. The ready sympathy of the cattleman had gone out to the politician who was down and out. He had heard the situation discussed enough to guess pretty close to the facts, and he could not let himself rest until he had made some effort to help the man whom his exposure had ruined, or, rather, had hastened to ruin, for that result had been for years approaching.

"I'm sorry, Mr. Pelton. If I've injured you I want to make it right."

"Make it right!" The former congressman got up with an oath. "Make it right! Can you give me back my reputation, my future? Can you take away the shame that has come upon my wife, and that my children will have to bear in the years to come? Can you give us back our home, our comfort, our peace of mind?"

"No, I can't do this, but I can help you to do it all," the cattleman made answer quietly.

He offered no defense, though he knew perfectly well none was needed. He had no responsibility in the calamity that had befallen this family. Pelton's wrong-doing had come home to those he loved, and he could rightly blame nobody but himself. However much he might arraign those who had been the agents of his fall, he knew in his heart that the fault had been his own.

Norma Pelton, tensely self-repressed, spoke now. "How can you do this, sir?"

"I can't do it so long as you hold me for an enemy, ma'am. I'm ready to cry quits with your husband and try a new deal. If I injured him he tried to even things up. Well, let's say things are squared and start fresh. I've got a business proposition to make if you're willing to listen to it."

"What sort of a proposition?"

"I'm running about twenty-five thousand sheep up in the hills. I've just bought a ranch with a comfortable ranch-house on it for a kind of central point. My winter feeding will all be done from it as a chief place of distribution. Same with the shearing and shipping. I want a good man to put in charge of my sheep as head manager, and I would be willing to pay a proper salary. There ain't any reason why this shouldn't work into a partnership if he makes good. With wool jumping, as it's going to do in the next four years, the right kind of man can make himself independent for life. My idea is to increase my holdings right along, and let my manager in as a partner as soon as he shows he is worth it. Now that ranch-house is a decent place. There's a pretty good school, ma'am, for the children. The folks round that neighborhood may not have any frills, but—"

"Are you offering Tom the place as manager?" she demanded, in amazement.

"That was my idea, ma'am. It's not what you been used to, o' course, but if you're looking for a change I thought I'd speak of it," he said diffidently.

She looked at him in a dumb surprise. She, too, in her heart knew that this man was blameless. He had done his duty, and had nearly lost his life for it at the hands of her husband. Now, he had come to lift them out of the hideous nightmare into which they had fallen. He had come to offer them peace and quiet and plenty in exchange for the future of poverty and shame and despair which menaced them. They were to escape into God's great hills, away from the averted looks and whispering tongues and the temptations to drown his trouble that so constantly beset the father of her children. Despite his faults she still loved Tom Pelton; he was a kind and loving husband and father. Out on the range there still waited a future for him. When she thought of it a lump rose in her throat for very happiness. She, who had been like a rock beside him in his trouble, broke down now and buried her head in her husband's coat.

"Don't you, honey—now, don't you cry." The big man had lost all his pomposity, and was comforting his sweetheart as simply as a boy. "It's all been my fault. I've been doing wrong for years—trying to pull myself out of the mire by my bootstraps. By Gad, you're a man, Sam Yesler, that's what you are. If I don't turn ovah a new leaf I'd ought to be shot. We'll make a fresh start, sweetheart. Dash me, I'm nothing but a dashed baby." And with that the overwrought man broke down, too.

Yesler, moved a good deal himself, maintained the burden of the conversation cheerfully.

"That's all settled, then. Tell you I'm right glad to get a competent man to put in charge. Things have been running at loose ends, because I haven't the time to look after them. This takes a big load off my mind. You better arrange to go up there with me as soon as you have time, Pelton, and look the ground over. You'll want to make some changes if you mean to take your family up there. Better to spend a few hundreds and have things the way you want them for Mrs. Pelton than to move in with things not up to the mark. Of course, I'll put the house in the shape you want it. But we can talk of that after we look it over."

In his embarrassment he looked so much the boy, so much the culprit caught stealing apples and up for sentence, that Norma Pelton's gratitude took courage. She came across to him and held out both hands, the shimmer of tears still in the soft brown eyes.

"You've given us more than life, Mr. Yesler. You can't ever

know what you have done for us. Some things are worse than death to some people. I don't mean poverty, but—other things. We can begin again far away from this tainted air that has poisoned us. I know it isn't good form to be saying this. One shouldn't have feelings in public. But I don't care. I think of the children—and Tom. I didn't expect ever to be happy again, but we shall. I feel it."

She broke down again and dabbed at her eyes with her kerchief. Sam, very much embarrassed but not at all displeased at this display of feeling, patted her dark hair and encouraged her to composure.

"There. It's all right, now, ma'am. Sure you'll be happy. Any mother that's got kids like these—"

He caught up the little girl in his arms by way of diverting attention from himself.

This gave a new notion to the impulsive little woman.

"I want you to kiss them both. Come here, Kennie. This is Mr. Yesler, and he is the best man you've ever seen. I want you to remember that he has been our best friend."

"Yes, mama."

"Oh, sho, ma'am!" protested the overwhelmed cattleman, kissing both the children, nevertheless.

Pelton laughed. He felt a trifle hysterical himself. "If she thinks it she'll say it when she feels that way. I'm right surprised she don't kiss you, too."

"I will," announced Norma promptly, with a pretty little tide of color.

She turned toward him, and Yesler, laughing, met the red lips of the new friend he had made.

"Now, you've got just grounds for shooting me," he said gaily, and instantly regretted his infelicitous remark

For both husband and wife fell grave at his words. It was Pelton that answered them.

"I've been taught a lesson, Mr. Yesler. I'm never going to pack a gun again as long as I live, unless I'm hunting or something of that sort, and I'm never going to drink another drop of liquor. It's all right for some men, but it isn't right for me."

"Glad to hear it. I never did believe in the hip-pocket habit. I've lived here twenty years, and I never found it necessary except on special occasions. When it comes to whisky, I reckon we'd all be better without it."

Yesler made his escape at the earliest opportunity and left them alone together. He lunched at the club, attended to some correspondence he had, and about 3:30 drifted down the street toward the post-office. He had expectations of meeting a young woman who often passed about that time on her way home from school duties.

It was, however, another young woman whose bow he met in front of Mesa's largest department store.

"Good afternoon, Miss Balfour."

She nodded greeting and cast eyes of derision on him.

"I've been hearing about you. Aren't you ashamed of yourself?"

"Yes, ma'am. What for in particular? There are so many things."

"You're a fine Christian, aren't you?" she scoffed.

"I ain't much of a one. That's a fact," he admitted. "What is it this time—poker?"

"No, it isn't poker. Worse than that. You've been setting a deplorable example to the young."

"To young ladies—like Miss Virginia?" he wanted to know.

"No, to young Christians. I don't know what our good deacons will say about it." She illuminated her severity with a flashing smile. "Don't you know that the sins of the fathers are to descend upon their children even to the third and fourth generation? Don't you know that when a man does wrong he must die punished, and his children and his wife, of course, and that the proper thing to do is to stand back and thank Heaven we haven't been vile sinners?"

"Now, don't you begin on that, Miss Virginia," he warned.

"And after the man had disgraced himself and shot you, after all respectable people had given him an extra kick to let him know he must stay down and had then turned their backs upon him. I'm not surprised that you're ashamed."

"Where did you get hold of this fairy-tale?" he plucked up courage to demand.

"From Norma Pelton. She told me everything, the whole story from beginning to end."

"It's right funny you should be calling on her, and you a

respectable young lady—unless you went to deliver that extra kick you was mentioning," he grinned.

She dropped her raillery. "It was splendid. I meant to ask Mr. Ridgway to do something for them, but this is so much better. It takes them away from the place of his disgrace and away from temptation. Oh, I don't wonder Norma kissed you."

"She told you that, too, did she?"

"Yes. I should have done it, too, in her place."

He glanced round placidly. "It's a right public place here, but—"

"Don't be afraid. I'm not going to." And before she disappeared within the portals of the department store she gave him one last thrust. "It's not so public up in the library. Perhaps if you happen to be going that way "

She left her communication a fragment, but he thought it worth acting upon. Among the library shelves he found Laska deep in a new volume on domestic science.

"This ain't any kind of day to be fooling away your time on cook-books. Come out into the sun and live," he invited.

They walked past the gallows-frames and the slag-dumps and the shaft-houses into the brown hills beyond the point where green copper streaks showed and spurred the greed of man. It was a day of spring sunshine, the good old earth astir with her annual recreation. The roadside was busy with this serious affair of living. Ants and crawling things moved to and fro about their business. Squirrels raced across the road and stood up at a safe distance to gaze at these intruders.

Birds flashed back and forth, hurried little carpenters busy with the specifications for their new nests. Eager palpitating life was the key-note of the universe.

"Virginia told me about the Peltons," Laska said, after a pause.

"It's spreading almost as fast as if it were a secret," he smiled. "I'm expecting to find it in the paper when we get back."

"I'm so glad you did it."

"Well, you're to blame."

"I!" She looked at him in surprise.

"Partly. You told me how things were going with them. That seemed to put it up to me to give Pelton a chance."

"I certainly didn't mean it that way. I had no right to ask you to do anything about it."

"Mebbe it was the facts put it up to me. Anyhow, I felt responsible."

"Mr. Roper once told me that you always feel responsible when you hear anybody is in trouble," the young woman answered.

"Roper's a goat. Nobody ever pays any attention to him."

Presently they diverged from the road and sat down on a great flat rock which dropped out from the hillside like a park seat. For he was still far from strong and needed frequent rests. Their talk was desultory, for they had reached that stage of friendship at which it is not necessary to bridge silence with idle small talk. Here, by some whim of fate, the word was spoken. He knew he loved her, but he had not meant to say it yet.

But when her steady gray eyes came back to his after a long stillness, the meeting brought him a strange feeling that forced his hand.

"I love you, Laska. Will you be my wife?" he asked quietly.

"Yes, Sam," she answered directly. That was all. It was settled with a word. There in the sunshine he kissed her and sealed the compact, and afterward, when the sun was low among the hill spurs, they went back happily to take up again the work that awaited them.

CHAPTER 25

FRIENDLY ENEMIES

Ridgway had promised Aline that he would see her soon, and when he found himself in New York he called at the big house on Fifth Avenue, which had for so long been identified as the home of Simon Harley. It bore his impress stamped on it. Its austerity suggested the Puritan rather than the classic conception of simplicity. The immense rooms were as chill as dungeons, and the forlorn little figure in black, lost in the loneliness of their bleakness, wandered to and fro among her retinue of servants like a butterfly beating its wings against a pane of glass.

With both hands extended she ran forward to meet her guest.

"I'm so glad, so glad, so glad to see you."

The joy-note in her voice was irrepressible. She had been alone for weeks with the conventional gloom that made an obsession of the shadow of death which enveloped the house. All voices and footsteps had been subdued to harmonize with the grief of the mistress of this mausoleum. Now she heard the sharp tread of this man unafraid, and saw the alert vitality of his confident bearing. It was like a breath of the hills to a parched traveler.

"I told you I would come."

"Yes. I've been looking for you every day. I've checked each one off on my calendar. It's been three weeks and five days since I saw you."

"I thought it was a year," he laughed, and the sound of his uncurbed voice rang strangely in this room given to murmurs.

"Tell me about everything. How is Virginia, and Mrs. Mott, and Mr. Yesler? And is he really engaged to that sweet little school-teacher? And how does Mr. Hobart like being senator?"

"Not more than a dozen questions permitted at a time. Begin again, please."

"First, then, when did you reach the city?"

He consulted his watch. "Just two hours and twenty-seven minutes ago."

"And how long are you going to stay?"

"That depends."

"On what?"

"For one thing, on whether you treat me well," he smiled.

"Oh, I'll treat you well. I never was so glad to see a real live somebody in my life. It's been pretty bad here." She gave a dreary little smile as she glanced around at the funereal air of the place. "Do you know, I don't think we think of death in the right way? Or, maybe, I'm a heathen and haven't the proper feelings."

She had sat down on one of the stiff divans, and Ridgway found a place beside her.

"Suppose you tell me about it," he suggested.

"I know I must be wrong, and you'll be shocked when you hear."

"Very likely."

"I can't help feeling that the living have rights, too," she began dubiously. "If they would let me alone I could be sorry in my own way, but I don't see why I have to make a parade of grief. It seems to—to cheapen one's feelings, you know."

He nodded. "Just as if you had to measure your friendship for the dead with a yardstick of Mother Grundy. It's a hideous imposition laid on us by custom, one of Ibsen's ghosts."

"It's so good to hear you say that. And do you think I may begin to be happy again?"

"I think it would be allowable to start with one smile a day, say, and gradually increase the dose," he jested. "In the course of a week, if it seems to agree with you, try a laugh."

She made the experiment without waiting the week, amused at his whimsical way of putting it. Nevertheless, the sound of her own laughter gave her a little shock.

"You came on business, I suppose?" she said presently.

"Yes. I came to raise a million dollars for some improvements

I want to make."

"Let me lend it to you," she proposed eagerly.

"That would be a good one. I'm going to use it to fight the Consolidated. Since you are now its chief stockholder you would be letting me have money with which to fight you."

"I shouldn't care about that. I hope you beat me."

"You're my enemy now. That's not the way to talk." His eyes twinkled merrily.

"Am I your enemy? Let's be friendly enemies, then. And there's something I want to talk to you about. Before he died Mr. Harley told me he had made you an offer. I didn't understand the details, but you were to be in charge of all the copper-mines in the country. Wasn't that it?"

"Something of that sort. I declined the proposition."

"I want you to take it now and manage everything for me. I don't know Mr. Harley's associates, but I can trust you. You can arrange it any way you like, but I want to feel that you have the responsibility."

He saw again that vision of power—all the copper interests of the country pooled, with himself at the head of the combination. He knew it would not be so easy to arrange as she thought, for, though she had inherited Harley's wealth, she had not taken over his prestige and force. There would be other candidates for leadership. But if he managed her campaign Aline's great wealth must turn the scale in their favor.

"You must think this over again. You must talk it over with

your advisers before we come to a decision," he said gravely.

"I've told Mr. Jarmyn. He says the idea is utterly impossible. But we'll show him, won't we? It's my money and my stock, not his. I don't see why he should dictate. He's always 'My dear ladying' me. I won't have it," she pouted.

The fighting gleam was in Ridgway's eyes now. "So Mr. Jannyn thinks it is impossible, does he?"

"That's what he said. He thinks you wouldn't do at all."

"If you really mean it we'll show him about that."

She shook hands with him on it.

"You're very good to me," she said, so naively that he could not keep back his smile.

"Most people would say I was very good to myself. What you offer me is a thing I might have fought for all my life and never won."

"Then I'm glad if it pleases you. That's enough about business. Now, we'll talk about something important."

He could think of only one thing more important to him than this, but it appeared she meant plans to see as much as possible of him while he was in the city.

"I suppose you have any number of other friends here that will want you?" she said.

"They can't have me if this friend wants me," he answered, with that deep glow in his eyes she recognized from of old; and before she could summon her reserves of defense he asked: "Do you want me, Aline?"

His meaning came to her with a kind of sweet shame. "No, no, no—not yet," she cried.

"Dear," he answered, taking her little hand in his big one, "only this now: that I can't help wanting to be near you to comfort you, because I love you. For everything else, I am content to wait."

"And I love you," the girl-widow answered, a flush dyeing her cheeks. "But I ought not to tell you yet, ought I?"

There was that in her radiant tear-dewed eyes that stirred the deepest stores of tenderness in the man. His finer instincts, vandal and pagan though he was, responded to it.

"It is right that you should tell me, since it is true, but it is right, too, that we should wait."

"It is sweet to know that you love me. There are so many things I don't understand. You must help me. You are so strong and so sure, and I am so helpless."

"You dear innocent, so strong in your weakness," he murmured to himself.

"You must be a guide to me and a teacher."

"And you a conscience to me," he smiled, not without amusement at the thought.

She took it seriously. "But I'm afraid I can't. You know so much better than I do what is right."

"I'm quite a paragon of virtue," he confessed.

"You're so sure of everything. You took it for granted that I loved you. Why were you so sure?"

"I was just as sure as you were that I cared for you. Confess."

She whispered it. "Yes, I knew it, but when you did not come I thought, perhaps You see, I'm not strong or clever. I can't help you as Virginia could." She stopped, the color washing from her face. "I had forgotten. You have no right to love me—nor I you," she faltered.

"Girl o'mine, we have every right in the world. Love is never wrong unless it is a theft or a robbery. There is nothing between me and Virginia that is not artificial and conventional, no tie that ought not to be broken, none that should ever of right have existed. Love has the right of way before mere convention a hundredfold."

"Ah! If I were sure."

"But I was to be a teacher to you and a judge for you."

"And I was to be a conscience to you."

"But on this I am quite clear. I can be a conscience to myself. However, there is no hurry. Time's a great solvent."

"And we can go on loving each other in the meantime."

He lifted her little pink fingers and kissed them. "Yes, we can do that all the time."

CHAPTER 26

BREAKS ONE AND MAKES
ANOTHER ENGAGEMENT

Miss Balfour's glass made her irritably aware of cheeks unduly flushed and eyes unusually bright. Since she prided herself on being sufficient for the emergencies of life, she cast about in her mind to determine which of the interviews that lay before her was responsible for her excitement. It was, to be sure, an unusual experience for a young woman to be told that her fiance would be unable to marry her, owing to a subsequent engagement, but she looked forward to it with keen anticipation, and would not have missed it for the world. Since she pushed the thought of the other interview into the background of her mind and refused to contemplate it at all, she did not see how that could lend any impetus to her pulse.

But though she was pleasantly excited as she swept into the reception-room, Ridgway was unable to detect the fact in her cool little nod and frank, careless handshake. Indeed, she looked so entirely mistress of herself, so much the perfectly gowned exquisite, that he began to dread anew the task he had set himself. It is not a pleasant thing under the most favorable circumstances to beg off from marrying a young woman one has engaged oneself to, and Ridgway did not find it easier because the young woman looked every inch a queen, and was so manifestly far from suspecting the object of his call. "I haven't had a chance to congratulate you personally yes," she said, after they had drifted to chairs. "I've been immensely proud of you."

"I got your note. It was good of you to write as soon as you heard."

She swept him with one of her smile-lit side glances. "Though, of course, in a way, I was felicitating myself when I congratulated you."

"You mean?"

She laughed with velvet maliciousness. "Oh, well, I'm dragged into the orbit of your greatness, am I not? As the wife of the president of the Greater Consolidated Copper Company—the immense combine that takes in practically all the larger copper properties in the country—I should come in for a share of reflected glory, you know."

Ridgway bit his lip and took a deep breath, but before he had found words she was off again. She had no intention of letting him descent from the rack yet.

"How did you do it? By what magic did you bring it about? Of course, I've read the newspapers' accounts, seen your features and your history butchered in a dozen Sunday horrors, and thanked Heaven no enterprising reporter guessed enough to use me as copy. Every paper I have picked up for weeks has been full of you and the story of how you took Wall Street by the throat. But I suspect they were all guesses, merely superficial rumors except as to the main facts. What I want to know is the inside story—the lever by means of which you pried open the door leading to the inner circle of financial magnates. You have often told me how tightly barred that door is. What was the open-sesame you used as a countersign to make the keeper of the gate unbolt?

He thought he saw his chance. "The countersign was 'Aline Harley,'" he said, and looked her straight in the face. He wished he could find some way of telling her without making him feel so like a cad.

She clapped her hands. "I thought so. She backed you with that uncounted fortune her husband left her. Is that it?"

That is it exactly. She gave me a free hand, and the immense fortune she inherited from Harley put me in a position to force recognition from the leaders. After that it was only a question of time till I had convinced them my plan was good." He threw back his shoulders and tried to take the fence again. "Would you like to know why Mrs. Harley put her fortune at my command?"

"I suppose because she is interested in us and our little affair. Doesn't all the world love a lover?" she asked, with a disarming candor.

"She had a better reason," he said, meeting her eyes gravely.

"You must tell me it—but not just yet. I have something to tell you first." She held out her little clenched hand. "Here is something that belongs to you. Can you open it?"

He straightened her fingers one by one, and took from her palm the engagement-ring he had given her. Instantly he looked up, doubt and relief sweeping his face.

"Am I to understand that you terminate our engagement?"

She nodded.

"May I ask why?"

"I couldn't bring myself to it, Waring. I honestly tried, but I couldn't do it."

"When did you find this out?"

"I began to find it out the first day of our engagement. I couldn't make it seem right. I've been in a process of learning it ever since. It wouldn't be fair to you for me to marry you."

"You're a brick, Virginia!" he cried jubilantly.

"No, I'm not. That is a minor reason. The really important one is that it wouldn't be fair to me."

"No, it would not," he admitted, with an air of candor.

"Because, you see, I happen to care for another man," she purred.

His vanity leaped up fully armed. "Another man! Who?"

"That's my secret," she answered, smiling at his chagrin.

"And his?"

"I said mine. At any rate, if three knew, it wouldn't be a secret," was her quick retort.

"Do you think you have been quite fair to me, Virginia?" he asked, with gloomy dignity.

"I think so," she answered, and touched him with the riposte:

"I'm ready now to have you tell me when you expect to marry Aline Harley."

His dignity collapsed like a pricked bladder. "How did you know?" he demanded, in astonishment.

"Oh well, I have eyes."

"But I didn't know—I thought—"

"Oh, you thought! You are a pair of children at the game," this thousand-year-old young woman scoffed. "I have known for months that you worshiped each other."

"If you mean to imply " he began severely.

"Hit somebody of your size, Warry," she interrupted cheerfully, as to an infant. "If you suppose I am so guileless as not to know that you were coming here this afternoon to tell me you were regretfully compelled to give me up on account of a more important engagement, then you conspicuously fail to guess right. I read it in your note."

He gave up attempting to reprove her. It did not seem feasible under the circumstances. Instead, he held out the hand of peace, and she took it with a laugh of gay camaraderie.

"Well," he smiled, "it seems possible that we may both soon be subjects for congratulation. That just shows how things work around right. We never would have suited each other, you know."

"I'm quite sure we shouldn't," agreed Virginia promptly. "But I don't think I'll trouble you to congratulate me till you see me wearing another solitaire."

"We'll hope for the best," he said cheerfully. "If it is the man I think, he is a better man than I am."

"Yes, he is," she nodded, without the least hesitation.

"I hope you will be happy with him."

"I'm likely to be happy without him."

"Not unless he is a fool."

"Or prefers another lady, as you do."

She settled herself back in the low easy chair, with her hands clasped behind her head.

"And now I'd like to know why you prefer her to me," she demanded saucily. "Do you think her handsomer?"

He looked her over from the rippling brown hair to the trim suede shoes. "No," he smiled; "they don't make them handsomer."

"More intellectual?"

"No."

"Of a better disposition?"

"I like yours, too."

"More charming?"

"I find her so, saving your presence." "Please justify yourself in detail." He shook his head, still smiling. "My justification is not to be itemized. It lies deeper—in destiny, or fate, or whatever one calls it."

"I see." She offered Markham's verses as an explanation:

"Perhaps we are led and our loves are fated, And our steps are counted one by one; Perhaps we shall meet and our souls be mated, After the burnt-out sun."

"I like that. Who did you say wrote it?"

The immobile butler, as once before, presented a card for her inspection. Ridgway, with recollections of the previous occasion, ventured to murmur again: "The fairy prince."

Virginia blushed to her hair, and this time did not offer the card for his disapproval.

"Shall I congratulate him?" he wanted to know.

The imperious blood came to her cheeks on the instant. The sudden storm in her eyes warned him better than words.

"I'll be good," he murmured, as Lyndon Hobart came into the room.

His goodness took the form of a speedy departure. She followed him to the door for a parting fling at him.

"In your automobile you may reach a telegraph-office in about five minutes. With luck you may be engaged inside of an hour."

"You have the advantage of me by fifty-five minutes," he flung back.

"You ought to thank me on your knees for having saved you

a wretched scene this afternoon," was the best she could say to cover her discomfiture.

"I do. I do. My thanks are taking the form of leaving you with the prince."

"That's very crude, sir—and I'm not sure it isn't impertinent."

Miss Balfour was blushing when she returned to Hobart. He mistook the reason, and she could not very well explain that her blushes were due to the last wordless retort of the retiring "old love," whose hand had gone up in a ridiculous bless-you-my-children attitude just before he left her.

Their conversation started stiffly. He had come, he explained, to say good-by. He was leaving the State to go to Washington prior to the opening of the session.

This gave her a chance to congratulate him upon his election. "I haven't had an opportunity before. You've been so busy, of course, preparing to save the country, that your time must have been very fully occupied."

He did not show his surprise at this interpretation of the fact that he had quietly desisted from his attentions to her, but accepted it as the correct explanation, since she had chosen to offer it.

Miss Balfour expressed regret that he was going, though she did not suppose she would see any less of him than she had during the past two months. He did not take advantage of her little flings to make the talk less formal, and Virginia, provoked at his aloofness, offered no more chances. Things went very badly, indeed, for ten minutes, at the end of which time Hobart rose to go. Virginia was miserably aware of being wretched despite the cool hauteur of her seeming indifference. But he was too good a sportsman to go without letting her know he held no grudge.

"I hope you will be very happy with Mr. Ridgway. Believe me, there is nobody whose happiness I would so rejoice at as yours."

"Thank you," she smiled coolly, and her heart raced. "May I hope that your good wishes still obtain even though I must seek my happiness apart from Mr. Ridgway?"

He held her for an instant's grave, astonished questioning, before which her eyes fell. Her thoughts side-tracked swiftly to long for and to dread what was coming.

"Am I being told—you must pardon me if I have misunderstood your meaning—that you are no longer engaged to Mr. Ridgway?"

She made obvious the absence of the solitaire she had worn.

Before the long scrutiny of his steady gaze: her eyes at last fell.

"If you don't mind, I'll postpone going just yet," he said quietly.

Her racing heart assured her fearfully, delightfully, that she did not mind at all.

"I have no time and no compass to take my bearings. You will pardon me if what I say seems presumptuous?"

Silence, which is not always golden, oppressed her. Why could she not make light talk as she had been wont to do with Waring Ridgway?

William MacLeod Raine

"But if I ask too much, I shall not be hurt if you deny me," he continued. "For how long has your engagement with Mr. Ridgway been broken, may I ask?"

"Between fifteen and twenty minutes."

"A lovers' quarrel, perhaps!" he hazarded gently.

"On the contrary, quite final and irrevocable Mr. Ridgway and I have never been lovers. She was not sure whether this last was mean as a confession or a justification.

"Not lovers?" He waited for her to explain Her proud eyes faced him. "We became engaged for other reasons. I thought that did not matter. But I find my other reasons were not sufficient. To-day I terminated the engagement. But it is only fair to say that Mr. Ridgway had come here for that purpose. I merely anticipated him." Her self-contempt would not let her abate one jot of the humiliating truth. She flayed herself with a whip of scorn quite lost on Hobart.

A wave of surging hope was flushing his heart, but he held himself well in hand.

"I must be presumptuous still," he said. "I must find out if you broke the engagement because you care for another man?"

She tried to meet his shining eyes and could not. "You have no right to ask that."

"Perhaps not till I have asked something else. I wonder if I should have any chance if I were to tell you that I love you?"

Her glance swept him shyly with a delicious little laugh. You never can tell till you try."

Choose from Thousands of 1stWorldLibrary Classics By

A. M. Barnard
Ada Leverson
Adolphus William Ward
Aesop
Agatha Christie
Alexander Aaronsohn
Alexander Kielland
Alexandre Dumas
Alfred Gatty
Alfred Ollivant
Alice Duer Miller
Alice Turner Curtis
Alice Dunbar
Allen Chapman
Alleyne Ireland
Ambrose Bierce
Amelia E. Barr
Amory H. Bradford
Andrew Lang
Andrew McFarland Davis
Andy Adams
Angela Brazil
Anna Alice Chapin
Anna Sewell
Annie Besant
Annie Hamilton Donnell
Annie Payson Call
Annie Roe Carr
Annonaymous
Anton Chekhov
Archibald Lee Fletcher
Arnold Bennett
Arthur C. Benson
Arthur Conan Doyle
Arthur M. Winfield
Arthur Ransome
Arthur Schnitzler
Arthur Train
Atticus
B.H. Baden-Powell
B. M. Bower
B. C. Chatterjee
Baroness Emmuska Orczy
Baroness Orczy
Basil King
Bayard Taylor
Ben Macomber
Bertha Muzzy Bower
Bjornstjerne Bjornson

Booth Tarkington
Boyd Cable
Bram Stoker
C. Collodi
C. E. Orr
C. M. Ingleby
Carolyn Wells
Catherine Parr Traill
Charles A. Eastman
Charles Amory Beach
Charles Dickens
Charles Dudley Warner
Charles Farrar Browne
Charles Ives
Charles Kingsley
Charles Klein
Charles Hanson Towne
Charles Lathrop Pack
Charles Romyn Dake
Charles Whibley
Charles Willing Beale
Charlotte M. Braeme
Charlotte M. Yonge
Charlotte Perkins Stetson
Clair W. Hayes
Clarence Day Jr.
Clarence E. Mulford
Clemence Housman
Confucius
Coningsby Dawson
Cornelis DeWitt Wilcox
Cyril Burleigh
D. H. Lawrence
Daniel Defoe
David Garnett
Dinah Craik
Don Carlos Janes
Donald Keyhoe
Dorothy Kilner
Dougan Clark
Douglas Fairbanks
E. Nesbit
E. P. Roe
E. Phillips Oppenheim
E. S. Brooks
Earl Barnes
Edgar Rice Burroughs
Edith Van Dyne
Edith Wharton

Edward Everett Hale
Edward J. O'Biren
Edward S. Ellis
Edwin L. Arnold
Eleanor Atkins
Eleanor Hallowell Abbott
Eliot Gregory
Elizabeth Gaskell
Elizabeth McCracken
Elizabeth Von Arnim
Ellem Key
Emerson Hough
Emilie F. Carlen
Emily Bronte
Emily Dickinson
Enid Bagnold
Enilor Macartney Lane
Erasmus W. Jones
Ernie Howard Pie
Ethel May Dell
Ethel Turner
Ethel Watts Mumford
Eugene Sue
Eugenie Foa
Eugene Wood
Eustace Hale Ball
Evelyn Everett-green
Everard Cotes
F. H. Cheley
F. J. Cross
F. Marion Crawford
Fannie E. Newberry
Federick Austin Ogg
Ferdinand Ossendowski
Fergus Hume
Florence A. Kilpatrick
Fremont B. Deering
Francis Bacon
Francis Darwin
Frances Hodgson Burnett
Frances Parkinson Keyes
Frank Gee Patchin
Frank Harris
Frank Jewett Mather
Frank L. Packard
Frank V. Webster
Frederic Stewart Isham
Frederick Trevor Hill
Frederick Winslow Taylor

Friedrich Kerst
Friedrich Nietzsche
Fyodor Dostoyevsky
G.A. Henty
G.K. Chesterton
Gabrielle E. Jackson
Garrett P. Serviss
Gaston Leroux
George A. Warren
George Ade
Geroge Bernard Shaw
George Cary Eggleston
George Durston
George Ebers
George Eliot
George Gissing
George MacDonald
George Meredith
George Orwell
George Sylvester Viereck
George Tucker
George W. Cable
George Wharton James
Gertrude Atherton
Gordon Casserly
Grace E. King
Grace Gallatin
Grace Greenwood
Grant Allen
Guillermo A. Sherwell
Guliclma Zollinger
Gustav Flaubert
H. A. Cody
H. B. Irving
H.C. Bailey
H. G. Wells
H. H. Munro
H. Irving Hancock
H. R. Naylor
H. Rider Haggard
H. W. C. Davis
Haldeman Julius
Hall Caine
Hamilton Wright Mabie
Hans Christian Andersen
Harold Avery
Harold McGrath
Harriet Beecher Stowe
Harry Castlemon
Harry Coghill
Harry Houidini

Hayden Carruth
Helent Hunt Jackson
Helen Nicolay
Hendrik Conscience
Hendy David Thoreau
Henri Barbusse
Henrik Ibsen
Henry Adams
Henry Ford
Henry Frost
Henry James
Henry Jones Ford
Henry Seton Merriman
Henry W Longfellow
Herbert A. Giles
Herbert Carter
Herbert N. Casson
Herman Hesse
Hildegard G. Frey
Homer
Honore De Balzac
Horace B. Day
Horace Walpole
Horatio Alger Jr.
Howard Pyle
Howard R. Garis
Hugh Lofting
Hugh Walpole
Humphry Ward
Ian Maclaren
Inez Haynes Gillmore
Irving Bacheller
Isabel Cecilia Williams
Isabel Hornibrook
Israel Abrahams
Ivan Turgenev
J.G.Austin
J. Henri Fabre
J. M. Barrie
J. M. Walsh
J. Macdonald Oxley
J. R. Miller
J. S. Fletcher
J. S. Knowles
J. Storer Clouston
J. W. Duffield
Jack London
Jacob Abbott
James Allen
James Andrews
James Baldwin

James Branch Cabell
James DeMille
James Joyce
James Lane Allen
James Lane Allen
James Oliver Curwood
James Oppenheim
James Otis
James R. Driscoll
Jane Abbott
Jane Austen
Jane L. Stewart
Janet Aldridge
Jens Peter Jacobsen
Jerome K. Jerome
Jessie Graham Flower
John Buchan
John Burroughs
John Cournos
John F. Kennedy
John Gay
John Glasworthy
John Habberton
John Joy Bell
John Kendrick Bangs
John Milton
John Philip Sousa
John Taintor Foote
Jonas Lauritz Idemil Lie
Jonathan Swift
Joseph A. Altsheler
Joseph Carey
Joseph Conrad
Joseph E. Badger Jr
Joseph Hergesheimer
Joseph Jacobs
Jules Vernes
Julian Hawthrone
Julie A Lippmann
Justin Huntly McCarthy
Kakuzo Okakura
Karle Wilson Baker
Kate Chopin
Kenneth Grahame
Kenneth McGaffey
Kate Langley Bosher
Kate Langley Bosher
Kathcrine Cecil Thurston
Katherine Stokes
L. A. Abbot
L. T. Meade

L. Frank Baum
Latta Griswold
Laura Dent Crane
Laura Lee Hope
Laurence Housman
Lawrence Beasley
Leo Tolstoy
Leonid Andreyev
Lewis Carroll
Lewis Sperry Chafer
Lilian Bell
Lloyd Osbourne
Louis Hughes
Louis Joseph Vance
Louis Tracy
Louisa May Alcott
Lucy Fitch Perkins
Lucy Maud Montgomery
Luther Benson
Lydia Miller Middleton
Lyndon Orr
M. Corvus
M. H. Adams
Margaret E. Sangster
Margret Howth
Margaret Vandercook
Margaret W. Hungerford
Margret Penrose
Maria Edgeworth
Maria Thompson Daviess
Mariano Azuela
Marion Polk Angellotti
Mark Overton
Mark Twain
Mary Austin
Mary Catherine Crowley
Mary Cole
Mary Hastings Bradley
Mary Roberts Rinehart
Mary Rowlandson
M. Wollstonecraft Shelley
Maud Lindsay
Max Beerbohm
Myra Kelly
Nathaniel Hawthrone
Nicolo Machiavelli
O. F. Walton
Oscar Wilde
Owen Johnson
P.G. Wodehouse
Paul and Mabel Thorne

Paul G. Tomlinson
Paul Severing
Percy Brebner
Percy Keese Fitzhugh
Peter B. Kyne
Plato
Quincy Allen
R. Derby Holmes
R. L. Stevenson
R. S. Ball
Rabindranath Tagore
Rahul Alvares
Ralph Bonehill
Ralph Henry Barbour
Ralph Victor
Ralph Waldo Emmerson
Rene Descartes
Ray Cummings
Rex Beach
Rex E. Beach
Richard Harding Davis
Richard Jefferies
Richard Le Gallienne
Robert Barr
Robert Frost
Robert Gordon Anderson
Robert L. Drake
Robert Lansing
Robert Lynd
Robert Michael Ballantyne
Robert W. Chambers
Rosa Nouchette Carey
Rudyard Kipling
Saint Augustine
Samuel B. Allison
Samuel Hopkins Adams
Sarah Bernhardt
Sarah C. Hallowell
Selma Lagerlof
Sherwood Anderson
Sigmund Freud
Standish O'Grady
Stanley Weyman
Stella Benson
Stella M. Francis
Stephen Crane
Stewart Edward White
Stijn Streuvels
Swami Abhedananda
Swami Parmananda
T. S. Ackland

T. S. Arthur
The Princess Der Ling
Thomas A. Janvier
Thomas A Kempis
Thomas Anderton
Thomas Bailey Aldrich
Thomas Bulfinch
Thomas De Quincey
Thomas Dixon
Thomas H. Huxley
Thomas Hardy
Thomas More
Thornton W. Burgess
U. S. Grant
Upton Sinclair
Valentine Williams
Various Authors
Vaughan Kester
Victor Appleton
Victor G. Durham
Victoria Cross
Virginia Woolf
Wadsworth Camp
Walter Camp
Walter Scott
Washington Irving
Wilbur Lawton
Wilkie Collins
Willa Cather
Willard F. Baker
William Dean Howells
William le Queux
W. Makepeace Thackeray
William W. Walter
William Shakespeare
Winston Churchill
Yei Theodora Ozaki
Yogi Ramacharaka
Young E. Allison
Zane Grey

www.ingramcontent.com/pod-product-compliance
Lightning Source LLC
Chambersburg PA
CBHW020616260626
47157CB00003B/1047